Things to
Make and Do

by DOUGLAS W. DOWNEY *and* KARIN WISIOL

Graphic design by Yvonne Beckwith

Drawings by Dick Fickle

STANDARD EDUCATIONAL CORPORATION *Chicago 1993*

Projects Created by: Esther M. Bjoland,
Douglas W. Downey, Ren Downey, Kenneth
Fitzpatrick, Sandra Fitzpatrick, Anne
Neigoff, Eugenia Pawlykowycz, Mathilda
Schirmer, Harriet Thompson, and
Karin Wisiol.

Testing Supervised by: Sandra Fitzpatrick.

Educational Consultant: Harry Bricker, Ph.D.

Technical Consultants: A bunch of kids
from Chicago, Glenview, and Northbrook,
Illinois.

Photographs by: Douglas W. Downey, Yvonne
Beckwith, Charles Malefyt, and John
Von Dorn.

Models: Daniele Almaraz, Frankie Anderson,
Drew Cuncannan, Paula Deleasco, Ren Downey,
Tommy Furtek, Anthony Hobart, Baron Hooper,
Holly Magie, Anne Malefyt, Mary Beth
Malefyt, Scott Osmon, Amy Peacock, Chuck
Peterson, Jason Redmond, Kelly Redmond,
Jennifer Rumpf, Betsy Schmidt, Benjamin
Stilp, Toby Sudduth, Sarah Williams,
and Frisky the Cat.

Library of Congress Cataloging in Publication Data
Downey, Douglas W   1929–
  Things to make and do.

  (Child horizons)
  First ed. by E. M. Bjoland published in 1952.
  1. Creative activities and seat work.
  I. Wisiol, Karin, 1935–   joint author.
  II. Bjoland, Esther M. Things to make and do.
  III. Title.
  LB1537.D65 1974   372.5'5   73–20249
  ISBN 0–87392–107–0

Introduction

THINGS TO MAKE AND DO is a completely new edition of a book first published in 1952. The most popular projects from the first edition have been redesigned and updated, but most of the projects are new. Some are originals, while others are old favorites. Some of the projects are of unknown origin—the authors learned of them from children who, in turn, learned of them from other children.

Handicrafts have a serious educational purpose—they channel creativity and aid in the development of manipulative skills. They'll fail in this purpose, however, unless they're fun . . . and unless they're workable. With this in mind, the authors and their associates examined hundreds of proposed projects to select ones that produce satisfying results with a minimum of difficulty. All of the projects were field-tested by parents and children. Out of this testing came the decision to write detailed, specific instructions and to use numerous step-by-step sketches. Some children won't need the instructions; they can work from the pictures alone. Others, however, will need the instructions to get them started. Once they have learned the basic techniques they will be able to make their own creations.

Many of the materials listed are household objects—paper bags and empty milk cartons, for example; the others are all inexpensive.

In the back of the book you will find several pages of useful information:

Spinning Pinwheel

Materials: typing paper; transparent tape; stick or ¼-inch dowel, at least 10 inches long; thumbtack. Tools: ruler; pencil; scissors; crayons or felt-tip markers.

A PINWHEEL is like a windmill—its arms are pushed around by the wind. To set it spinning, hold it in the wind, blow on it, or hold it up as you run. Here is how to make one:

Measure a 4-inch square on typing paper and cut it out. (Page 181 shows how.)

Draw two light lines across, from corner to corner. Number the corners 1, 2, 3, 4, exactly as shown in Drawing 1.

Draw a heavy X at the middle on the lines, about one inch long. Cut along the light lines, starting from the corners, just up to the X at the center.

Color each of the four sections a different color. Repeat the color on the back of each section or use a fifth color.

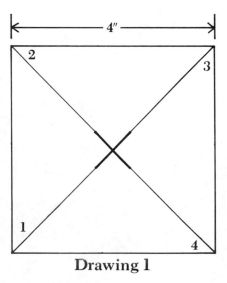

Drawing 1

5

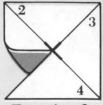

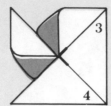

Drawing 2   **Drawing 3**

Drawing 4

Drawing 5

Take corner 1, place it over the center, and tape the tip in place. Drawing 2. Tape corner 2 on top of 1 (Drawing 3), corner 3 on top of 2 (Drawing 4), and corner 4 on top of 3.

Push a thumbtack through all four tips. Move the tack about to enlarge the hole slightly. Then push the tack into a stick or dowel 10 inches long (or longer), near the top of the stick. Drawing 5. Push it in just far enough so that it will hold. If you push it in too far the pinwheel won't spin.

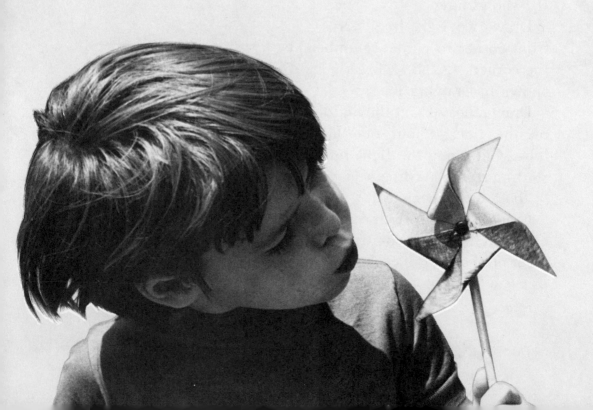

Paper Parachute

Materials: heavy thread; paper napkin; plastic soldier, plastic spool, chess piece, or cork. Tools: ruler; scissors.

PARACHUTES were invented to save lives, but they are also used in the sport called skydiving. Here is how you can skydive without ever leaving the ground:

Cut four pieces of thread, each 12 inches long. Tie one end of each thread to a corner of a paper napkin. Then tie the four loose ends together. See Drawing 1.

Cut a 6-inch length of thread and tie to the other threads at the point where they meet. To the other end of the 6-inch thread tie a plastic soldier, spool, or other small, lightweight object. Drawing 2.

Holding the parachute by the top center, throw it upward toward the ceiling and watch it float down.

7

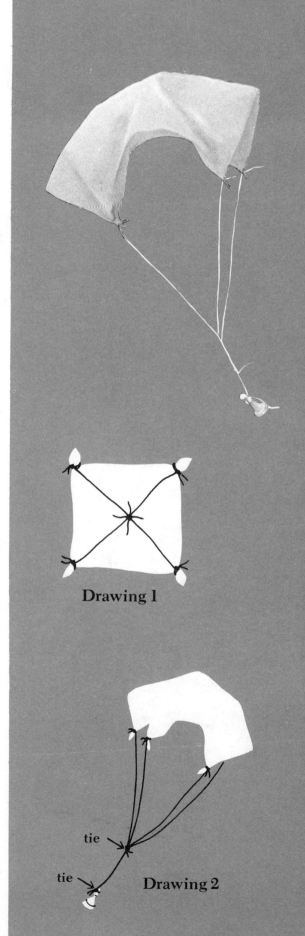

Drawing 1

tie

tie

Drawing 2

Paper Cutouts

Materials: newspapers to cover work space; typing paper or lightweight colored paper; tracing paper; masking tape; paste or white glue; lightweight cardboard. Tools: ruler; pencil; scissors. Optional: transparent tape.

PAPER THAT'S FOLDED before you cut it is full of surprises. You can make a chain of dolls holding hands and ready to dance. Or you can make a grove of Christmas trees.

This is how you make a chain of dolls:

Cut a strip of paper 11 inches long and 3¾ inches wide. (Page 180 shows how.) Fold the paper in half. See Drawing 1. Then fold each part in half, as in Drawing 2.

Place tracing paper over the

8

doll pattern, Drawing 3, and hold it in place with masking tape. Trace the pattern. Paste or glue the tracing to a piece of lightweight cardboard. Then cut it out. Lay the pattern on top of the folded paper and draw around it, making sure the doll's hands touch the edges of the paper. Drawing 4.

Hold the folds together tightly and cut out the doll. Do not cut where the doll's hands touch the edges.

Open the folded paper—and you have four dolls in a row, holding hands.

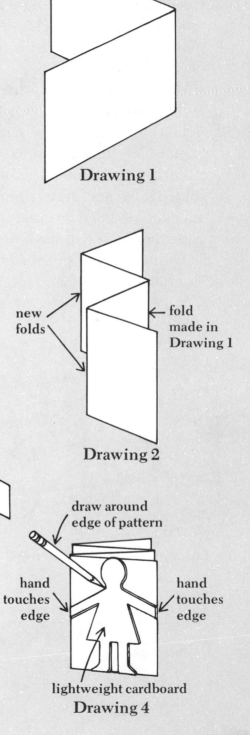

Drawing 1

new folds

fold made in Drawing 1

Drawing 2

pattern

Drawing 3

draw around edge of pattern

hand touches edge

hand touches edge

lightweight cardboard

Drawing 4

This is how you make a grove of Christmas trees:

Cut a strip of paper 11 inches long and 5 inches wide. Fold the paper in half and then fold one side in half again, folding inward. Drawing 5. Then fold in half again, this time folding outward. Drawing 6. Now fold in half once more, again folding outward. Drawing 7.

Do the same for the other side of the paper, so you will have eight folds in all. Drawing 8.

Trace the tree pattern, Drawing 9. Paste or glue the tracing to a piece of lightweight cardboard and cut it out. Place the pattern on the folded paper so that the tree trunk is on the folded edge and draw around it. Then cut out the tree, making sure you do not cut where the tree touches the edges. Open the paper and you will have four trees in a row.

To make a long chain of dolls or trees—first make several short chains and then tape the end of one chain to the next.

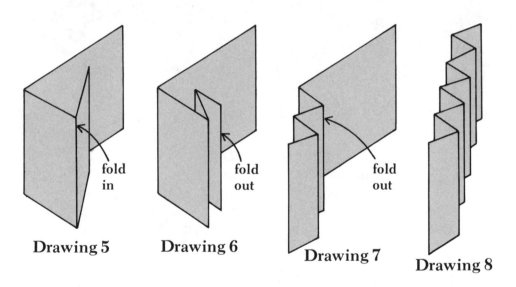

fold
in

Drawing 5

fold
out

Drawing 6

fold
out

Drawing 7

Drawing 8

this side goes over folded edge of paper

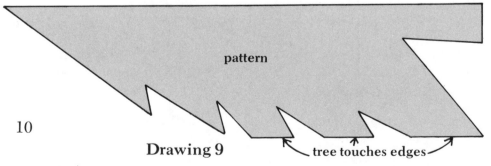

pattern

10

Drawing 9

tree touches edges

Bird Collage

Materials: newspapers to cover work space; shoe box cover; red poster paint; jar lid; plastic spoon; black paint and thinner (the kind used for plastic models); white glue; two plastic buttons; spout from salt box; plastic berry basket; tissue paper or crepe paper; two plastic forks. Tools: paintbrush; scissors.

SOME ARTISTS LIKE to make collages (rhymes with "garages" and "corsages"). These are arrangements of different kinds of things glued on a canvas or board. To put together this collage:

Paint a shoe box cover with red poster paint. Rinse your brush in water. Paint a jar lid and plastic spoon with the black paint. Let dry. Clean your brush with paint thinner.

Glue buttons (for eyes) and salt spout (beak) on the jar lid. From a plastic berry basket cut a piece for the head feathers and two pieces for the wings. Glue the three pieces on crepe or tissue paper. When they are dry, cut out around them.

Glue the jar lid and head feathers on the box lid as shown. Then glue on the plastic spoon, forks, and wings. The spoon and forks should be glued with the hollow sides down.

11

12

Koko
The Clown

Materials: newspapers to cover work space; tracing paper; masking tape; medium-weight cardboard; scraps of cloth; white glue. Tools: pencil; scissors; pins. Optional: carbon paper.

THE CIRCUS IS COMING! Make Koko some clown clothes. Then lean him up where he can practice his act for you. To get him ready:

Trace the outline of the clown and transfer the tracing to cardboard. (Pages 184 and 185 show how.) Cut out the cardboard figure.

Cut the shoes, suit, hat, gloves, and ball out of scraps of cloth. To get the right shapes, pin the tracing-paper drawing of the clown to the cloth. Then cut both the cloth and the tracing paper.

When the scraps are all cut out, glue them to the cardboard clown.

Monster Mask

Materials: newspapers to cover work space; paper bag big enough to fit over your head; two egg cartons; poster paint; white glue. Tools: scissors; felt-tip markers; pencil; paintbrush.

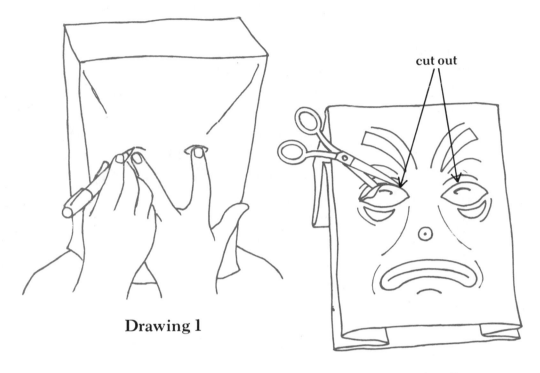

Drawing 1

cut out

Drawing 2

MASKS HAVE BEEN USED for as long as there have been people. Often dancers used them in acting out the part of an animal or spirit. Sometimes masks were used to scare evil spirits or children who didn't behave!

Halloween masks are scary just for fun. If you're not afraid of scaring yourself in a mirror, try this mask on.

Fit a paper bag over your head and trim it at the shoulders for a better fit.

With your fingers, gently feel where your eyes are. Mark the two spots on the bag with a felt-tip marker. See Drawing 1.

Take off the bag. Draw eyes around the two marks. Then draw the rest of the face and color it with felt-tip markers. Cut out the eye holes. Drawing 2.

Cut the covers off two egg cartons and discard the covers. Cut four egg compartments off the end of each carton. Drawing 3. Set these aside.

Then cut the other eight compartments of each carton in half the long way. Drawing 4.

Turn these over, hollow side down, and paint the bottoms. Drawing 5. When they are dry, glue two of these sections across the flat top of the mask, where hair belongs. Glue another one on the front of the mask, across the forehead. Glue another one on the front across the chin, as in the photograph on page 14.

From one of the carton ends that you cut off earlier, cut out one of the long, pointed sections between compartments. Drawing 6. Paint it and then glue it on the mask for a nose. Clean your paintbrush in water.

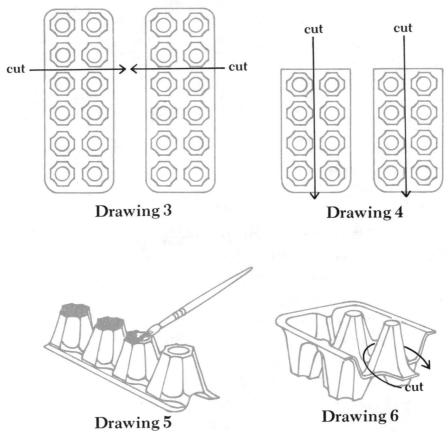

Drawing 3

Drawing 4

Drawing 5

Drawing 6

Peanut Shell Puppets

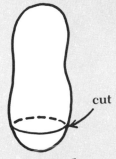

Drawing 1

Materials: peanuts.
Tools: scissors; felt-
tip marker.

Drawing 2

CAN YOU WIGGLE your fingers
and change your voice? Then
you can put on your own peanut play! To get your actors:

Choose a fairly straight pea-
nut like the one in the picture.
Cut off the bigger end. See
Drawing 1.

Shake the peanut out. (If the
hole is not large enough, trim
a little more off the end.)

When the nut is out, try to
fit the shell on one of your
fingers. Keep trimming a little
off the shell until it fits.

With a felt-tip marker, draw
two eyes, a nose, and a mouth
on the puppet. Drawing 2.

Make a second puppet for
another finger. Now your two
puppets can "talk" to each
other.

17

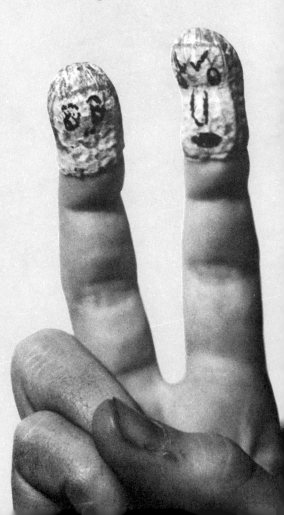

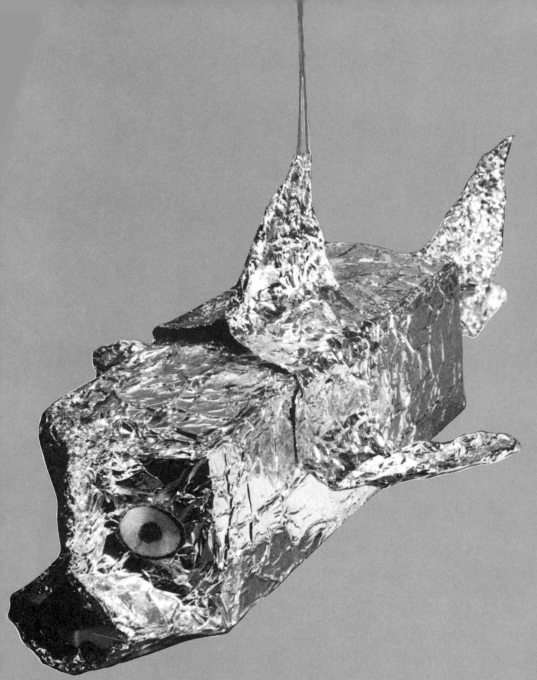

Spacefish

Materials: quart-size milk carton; heavy aluminum foil; transparent tape; construction paper; white glue; string. Tools: ruler; scissors; crayon; pencil.

SOME FISH LIVE DEEP in the ocean. Some live near the surface. And some—the flying fish—live in the ocean and in the air. Here's one that might live in space! To make Spacefish:

Open the pour spout of an empty quart-size milk carton. Cut a piece of aluminum foil about 15 inches long and 12 inches wide. (Page 180 shows how.) Wrap it around the carton and tape. Tuck the foil in around the spout. See Drawing 1.

Press the foil together flat in back to form a vertical tail fin. Pinch it together slightly near the body and push a notch into the end of it. Drawing 2.

If the foil around the body is still smooth, crinkle it here and there to give it a fishy look.

For fins, cut a piece of foil about 15 inches long and 4 inches wide. Fold both long edges to the middle. Then fold in half across the width. Drawing 3.

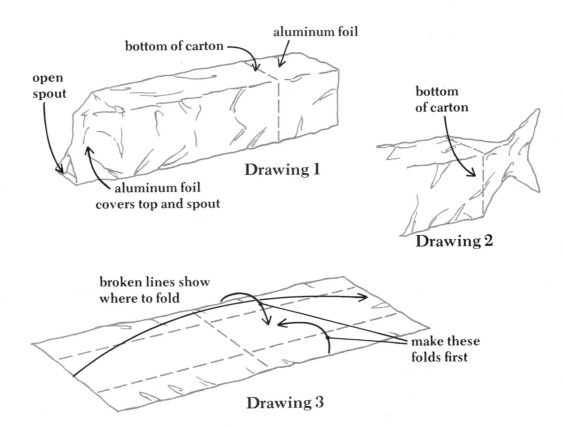

bottom of carton

aluminum foil

open spout

bottom of carton

aluminum foil covers top and spout

Drawing 1

Drawing 2

broken lines show where to fold

make these folds first

Drawing 3

Now fold over a corner at the middle and each end. Drawing 4. Bend the two ends up as in Drawing 5. Tape this piece over the fish's back with the fins sticking out. Drawing 6.

To make eyes, cut two nickel-size circles out of colored paper. Drawing 7. Color the edges and centers. Glue them above the fish's mouth. Drawing 8.

To hang Spacefish up, make a small hole with a pencil in its top fin and run a string through it. Your shower curtain rod might be a good place to hang it.

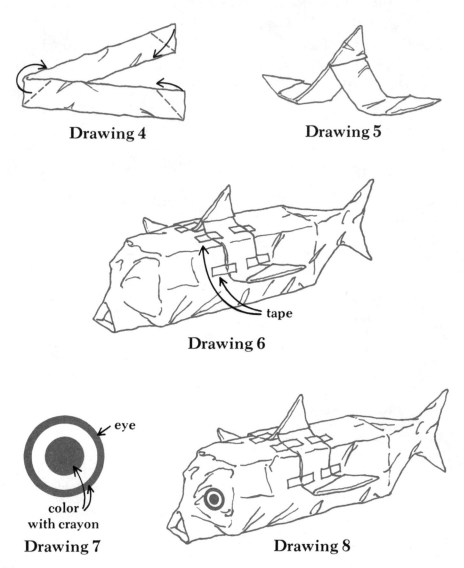

Drawing 4

Drawing 5

tape

Drawing 6

eye

color with crayon

Drawing 7

Drawing 8

Shadow Play

Needed: unshaded electric light or strong sunlight; blank area of wall.

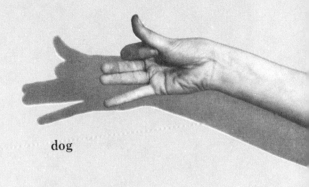

dog

IN THIS SHADOW THEATER, you are the director, producer, sound-effects man, and star. Be your own audience, too, until you're ready to give a grand show for your public.

Sit or stand between the light and the wall.

Look at the shadow dog shown here. Do you see how the upright thumb forms the dog's ear? how the bent index finger forms its forehead? and how the other fingers are spaced to form the open mouth? Hold your hand and fingers in the position shown. Watch the shadow you form. Move your fingers to make your dog come alive.

Now try to make the monster, the alligator, and the angel—or make up shadow pictures of your own.

21

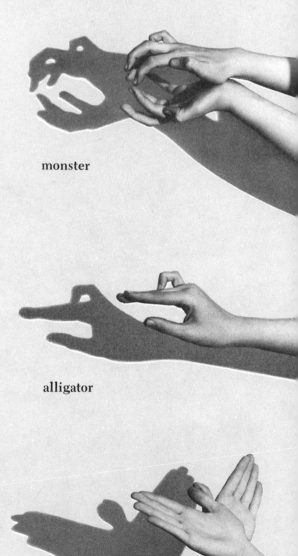

monster

alligator

angel

22

Box
Guitar

Materials: seven large rubber bands; cardboard box.

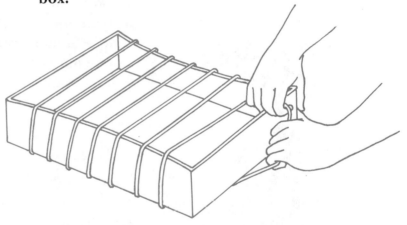

CAN YOU BEAT OUT THE RHYTHM of your favorite song? For a new sound, strum the rhythm on this guitar as you sing.

Find a box big enough to stretch rubber bands, but not so big that they will break. If the box has a top, remove it and discard.

Stretch rubber bands one by one around the box, spacing them to form strings, as shown in the drawing and the photograph.

When you strum your guitar with the open side up, you will hear a musical chord. When you strum it from the bottom, it will sound like a snare drum.

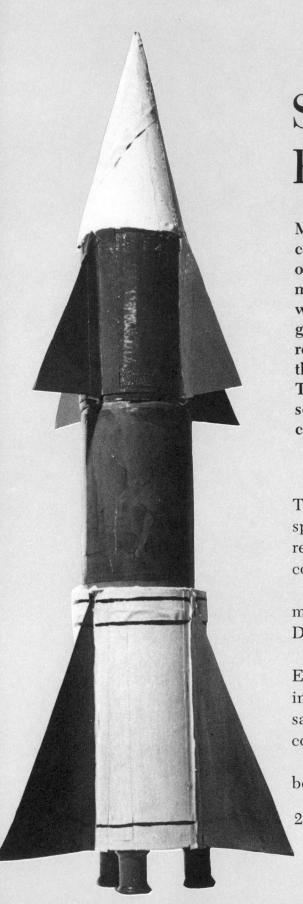

Space Rocket

Materials: newspapers to cover work space; round oatmeal or cornmeal box; masking tape; lightweight cardboard; white glue; salt box (for a super rocket, two salt boxes); three empty spools; paint. Tools: pencil; ruler; scissors; compass or other circle maker; paintbrush.

THE MOON? Mars? Pick your space target. To get your rocket ready for the launch pad and countdown:

Tape the cover onto an oatmeal or cornmeal box. See Drawing 1.

Cut four fins from cardboard. Each fin should be a triangle, 4 inches at the bottom and the same height as the oatmeal or cornmeal box. Drawing 2.

Glue and tape the fins to the box. Drawing 3.

24

On a piece of cardboard, draw a half circle with a 7-inch radius. (Page 182 shows how.) Drawing 4. Cut out the half circle and roll it into a cone. (Page 183 shows how.)

Adjust the bottom of the cone until it just fits the top of a salt box. Then tape the cone's seam and tape the cone to the box. Drawing 5.

Cut four cone fins from cardboard. The fins should be the same height as the side of the cone (or, for a super rocket, the same height as the salt box) and 3 inches wide at the bottom. Drawing 6.

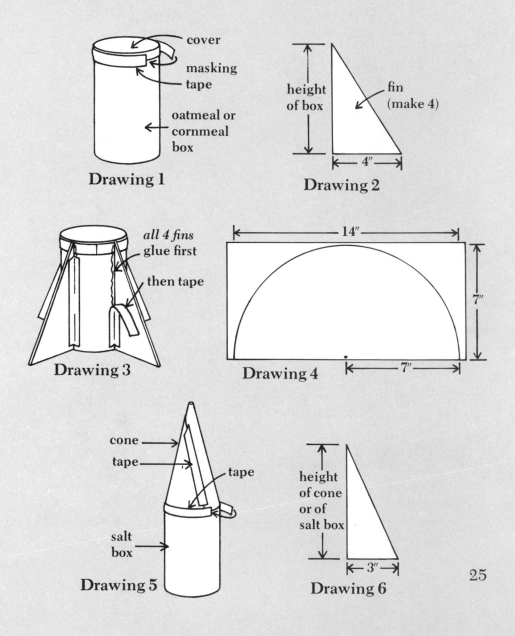

cover

masking tape

oatmeal or cornmeal box

Drawing 1

height of box

fin (make 4)

4"

Drawing 2

all 4 fins glue first

then tape

Drawing 3

14"

7"

7"

Drawing 4

cone

tape

tape

salt box

Drawing 5

height of cone or of salt box

3"

Drawing 6

25

Glue and tape the fins to the cone. Drawing 7. For a super rocket, attach the fins to the salt box instead. Then glue this salt box on top of a second salt box. Drawing 8.

Now glue the salt box (or boxes) to the oatmeal box, being careful to line up the top fins with the bottom fins. Drawings 9 and 10.

Glue three spools to the bottom of the oatmeal box. Drawing 11. These are your rocket's engines.

When the glue is dry, paint your rocket.

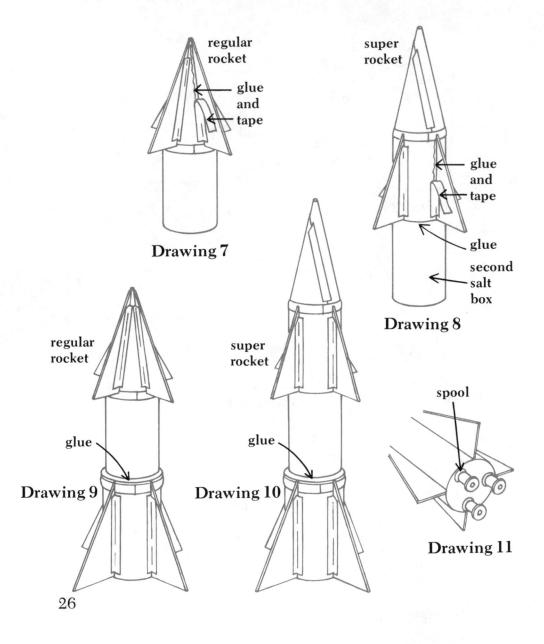

regular rocket
glue and tape

Drawing 7

super rocket
glue and tape
glue
second salt box

Drawing 8

regular rocket
glue

Drawing 9

super rocket
glue

Drawing 10

spool

Drawing 11

Musical Bottles

Needed: six pop bottles; pitcher of water; spoon.

MUSIC OUT OF BOTTLES? First, fill a bottle with water. Tap it lightly with a spoon and listen to the sound. Now pour some of the water out and tap the bottle again. Do you hear the change in the sound?

Pour different amounts of water into six bottles. Line them up in a row. Now tap each bottle lightly with the spoon. Can you play a song on the bottles?

You can change the sound each bottle makes by adding water or pouring some out.

Now blow across the top of each bottle. The one that had the lowest sound when you tapped it will have the highest sound now!

Paper Hat

Materials: newspaper, brown wrapping paper, or gift-wrapping paper. Tools: ruler; pencil; scissors. Optional: transparent tape.

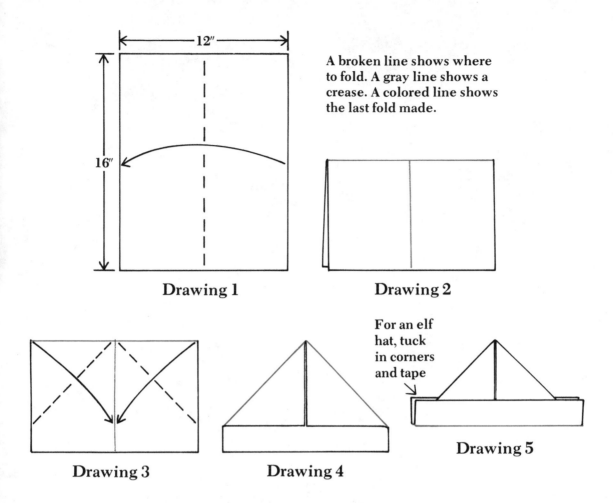

A broken line shows where to fold. A gray line shows a crease. A colored line shows the last fold made.

Drawing 1

Drawing 2

Drawing 3

Drawing 4

For an elf hat, tuck in corners and tape

Drawing 5

NEW HATS make people look different. Put a paper hat on, make a face, and guess who you are! When it's time for a party, make hats for everyone out of gift-wrapping paper.

Cut a piece of paper so that it measures 12 inches by 16 inches. (Page 180 shows how.) Fold the paper in half the long way to crease it. Then unfold it. See Drawing 1.

Now fold the paper in half across its width (so it measures 12 inches by 8 inches). Drawing 2.

Fold the top corners down to meet at the center crease. Drawings 3 and 4.

Fold the bottom up on each side to make the brim for a soldier hat. Drawing 5. If you want an elf hat (as in the photograph), tuck in the corners and tape. Now spread open the bottom and try on your hat!

29

Yarn Doll
Pin

Materials: medium-weight cardboard; yarn (two colors); safety pin.
Tools: pencil; ruler; scissors.

30

No danger of forgetting this doll—you can wear her!

Cut cardboard into a rectangle 3 inches by 6 inches. (Page 180 shows how.) Wind yarn around the cardboard the long way, about 30 times. See Drawing 1.

Slide the loops of yarn together at the top. Tie them together with a short piece of yarn run under the loops. Drawing 2. (Do all tying with a second color of yarn.)

To make arms, slide five or six strands of yarn off each side of the cardboard. Tie each bunch of strands together near the bottom with a short piece of yarn. Drawing 3.

Slide all of the yarn off the cardboard. To make a head, tie it together about 1 inch from the top with another piece of yarn. Stretch out the doll's arms and form a waist by tying the rest of the strands together with another piece of yarn about 3 inches from the top. Drawing 4.

Clip the loops of the folded-over yarn at the hands and skirt bottom. Drawing 5.

Attach with a safety pin to your favorite outfit.

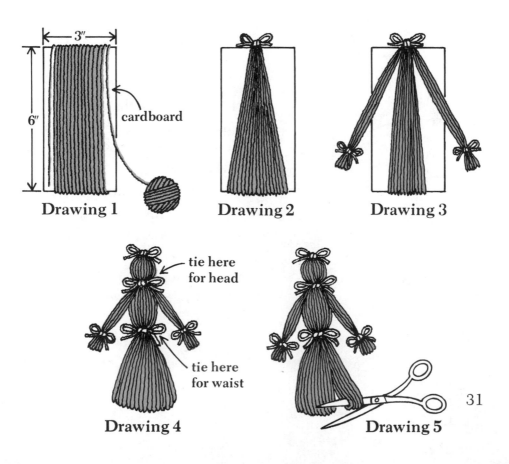

Drawing 1

3″

6″

cardboard

Drawing 2

Drawing 3

Drawing 4

tie here for head

tie here for waist

Drawing 5

31

Paper
Lanterns

Materials: construction paper; transparent tape; twine, narrow ribbon, or yarn. Tools: ruler; pencil; scissors.

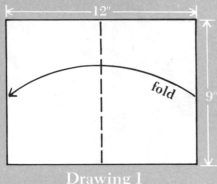

Drawing 1

LIKE BALLOONS, lanterns make a party look special. Try Halloween lanterns in orange, or birthday lanterns in many different colors. Hang a whole string of lanterns across the room. To make the first one:

Use a piece of construction paper 9 inches by 12 inches. Fold it in half lengthwise. See Drawing 1.

Draw a border 1½ inches from the open end. Drawing 2.

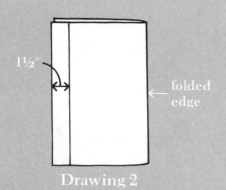

Drawing 2

Draw lines from the border line to the fold, about ½ inch apart. Drawing 3. Cut along these lines from the fold to the border.

Open up the paper and roll it into a cylinder. Drawing 4. The uncut borders should form the top and bottom. Tape together the two ends of the top border and then the two ends of the bottom border. Drawing 5.

Use a pencil to punch two holes, opposite each other, in the top border. Drawing 6. Thread twine, ribbon, or yarn through the holes. Make a knot or bow for hanging.

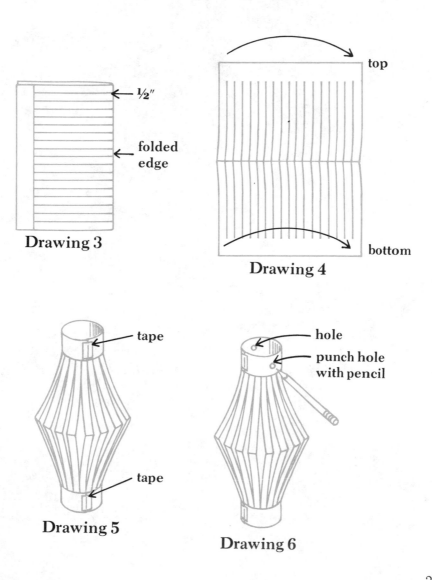

½"

folded edge

Drawing 3

top

bottom

Drawing 4

tape

tape

Drawing 5

hole

punch hole with pencil

Drawing 6

Dancing Clown
Puppet

Materials: tracing paper; masking tape; medium-weight cardboard. Tools: pencil; scissors; crayons or felt-tip markers. Optional: carbon paper.

HAVE YOU EVER TRIED to dance on your fingers? Here's a clown to show you how:

Trace the clown pattern. Transfer the tracing to a piece of cardboard. (Pages 184 and 185 show how.)

Ask an older person to help you cut out the leg holes of the cardboard clown.

Color him with crayons or felt-tip markers. Make the nose red.

Cut out your clown.

Now put two fingers through the leg holes. There —your clown has legs. Have him wiggle his legs and do a dance. He'll teach your fingers in a hurry!

leg hole   leg hole

Castle

Materials: newspapers to cover work space; box or carton measuring about 7 by 13 by 6 inches; two egg cartons; white glue; two quart-size milk cartons; gray, silver, or brown enamel paint; paint thinner; brown and yellow construction paper; transparent tape; two small frozen juice cans; four pipe cleaners; plastic berry basket; lightweight cardboard. **Tools:** scissors; ruler; pencil; paintbrush; dinner plate.

MANY HUNDREDS OF YEARS AGO, the kings and nobles of Europe built great castles that were homes and forts combined. Some are still standing. Their thick walls held against the battering ram. The drawbridge and portcullis (iron gate) protected the entrance. Iron bars closed off the windows. Soldiers standing at the battlements (walls on top with openings) shot arrows, darts, and stones at attackers. With enough food and weapons, the people of a well-built castle could hold off an attacking army for years.

Here is a castle you can build:

To form the castle building, use a box or carton about 7 by 13 by 6 inches. If you use a box, discard the cover. If you use a carton, tape the covers shut. Turn the box or carton upside down, so that the cover side is on the bottom.

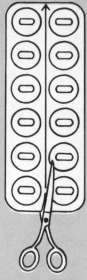

Drawing 1

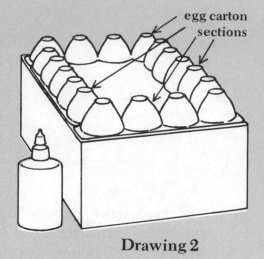

egg carton sections

Drawing 2

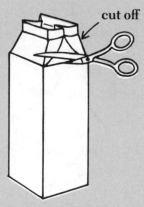

cut off

Drawing 3

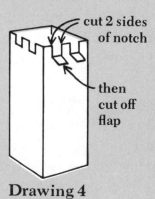

cut 2 sides of notch

then cut off flap

Drawing 4

To form battlements, cut the bottoms of two egg cartons in half the long way. See Drawing 1. (You'll need the tops later; save them.) Cut off the ends so they will fit on top of the castle and glue in place. Drawing 2.

To make square towers, open the tops of two quart-size milk cartons. Cut off and discard the top section of each. Drawing 3. Then cut notches about ¹/₂ inch deep and ¹/₂ inch wide all around the top edges of each carton. Drawing 4.

Paint the castle, battlements, and milk-carton towers with enamel paint. Clean your brush in thinner after you paint.

To make round towers, use brown construction paper and two small juice cans. Using a dinner plate as a guide, draw a half circle about 9 inches in diameter on one piece of construction paper. Drawing 5. Roll the paper into a cone whose base is the same size as the top of the can. (Page 183 shows how.) Tape the cone's seam. Glue the cone on top of one of the juice cans. Drawing 6. Now make a cone in the same way for the other can.

Measure and cut two strips of brown construction paper the same height as the height of the cans. Wrap a strip around each can. If the paper overlaps by more than an inch, cut off the excess. Glue or tape the paper in place. Drawing 7.

Make a pennant (a flag) for each round tower. First fold a piece of yellow construction paper in half and cut out a small triangle. Drawing 8. Then repeat using brown construction

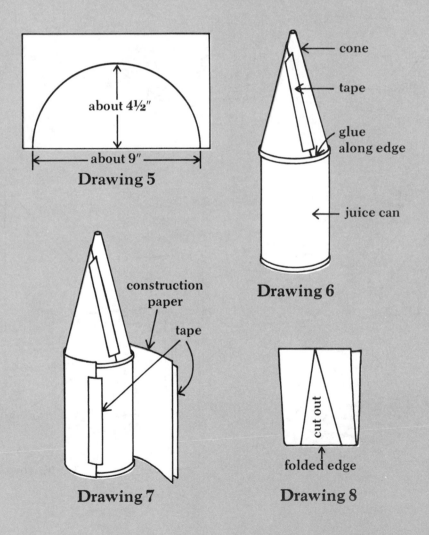

about 4½"

about 9"

Drawing 5

cone

tape

glue along edge

juice can

Drawing 6

construction paper

tape

Drawing 7

cut out

folded edge

Drawing 8

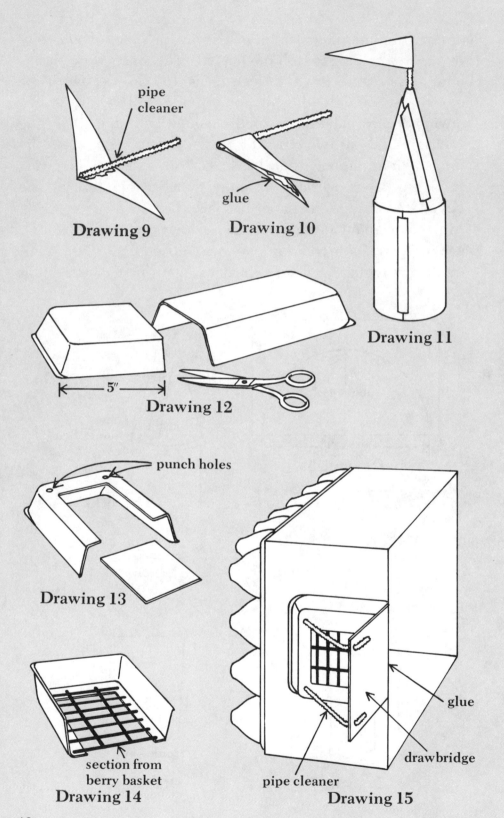

pipe
cleaner

Drawing 9

glue

Drawing 10

Drawing 11

5"

Drawing 12

punch holes

Drawing 13

section from
berry basket

Drawing 14

glue

drawbridge

pipe cleaner

Drawing 15

40

paper. Open the triangles. Glue a pipe cleaner near its end into the fold of each triangle. Drawing 9. Glue the triangles closed. Drawing 10. Insert the pipe cleaners into the cones. Drawing 11.

To make the castle entrance, cut across the top of an egg carton about 5 inches from one end. Drawing 12. Cut an arch in the center of this piece as shown in Drawing 13. Punch a hole high on each side of the piece with a pencil.

Cut a section from a plastic berry basket slightly larger than the arch. (Save the rest of the basket.) Glue the section on the arch from the back (the scooped-out side). Drawing 14. Glue the arch to the front of the castle.

To make a drawbridge, cut a rectangle from lightweight cardboard. Punch a hole in each corner at one end. Glue the end without holes under the arch. Insert pipe cleaners through the holes in the arch and the holes in the drawbridge. Bend the tips of the pipe cleaners under. Drawing 15.

Make windows on either side of the entrance by cutting two small rectangles out of the berry basket. Glue yellow paper to one side of the rectangles. Put glue on the paper side and glue the windows high up on each side of the entrance.

Stand the round towers on top of the castle and place or glue the square towers on either side of the entrance.

Make a Loom and Weave

Materials: medium-weight cardboard; yarn. Tools: ruler; pencil; scissors; paper punch.

IN MANY PARTS of the world, people make their cloth by weaving on a hand loom. This way of making cloth is thousands of years old. It is still used by craftsmen everywhere who want to make something especially fine.

Weave a coaster, place mat, doll blanket or rug, scarf, belt, or wall hanging.

Here's how to make your loom, as shown in Drawing 1:

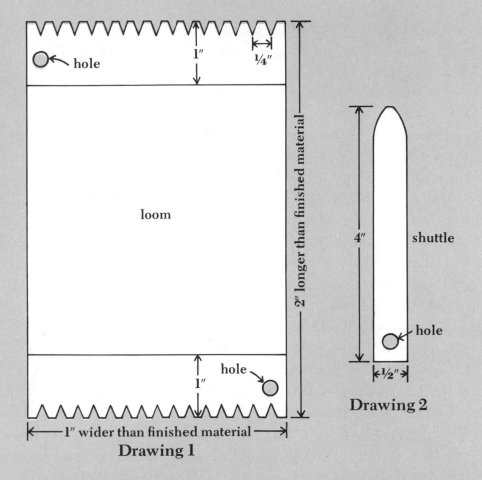

Drawing 1

Drawing 2

Decide how wide and how long you want your woven material to be. Draw a rectangle on cardboard 1 inch wider and 2 inches longer than the finished material. (Page 180 shows how.) Cut out the rectangle. Draw a line across the width 1 inch from each end.

Make an *odd* number of marks along the top and bottom edges, ¼ inch apart. Cut notches at the marks as shown at the top right corner of Drawing 1.

Punch a hole near the top left corner and bottom right corner.

On cardboard, draw a rectangle ½ inch wide and 4 inches long. Cut it out, making one end rounded. Then punch a hole near the other end. Drawing 2. This is your shuttle.

Tie one end of a piece of yarn to the top hole of the loom. Wind the yarn up and down between the notches. There are

43

two ways of doing this, as shown in Drawing 3. The first method is easier, but it wastes yarn, since the yarn on the back is later cut off and discarded.

Tie the yarn at the bottom hole. This yarn forms the *warp* threads of your material. Drawing 4.

The crosswise threads are called the *woof.* For these, you will need a long piece of yarn. Thread one end through the hole in the shuttle and tie it in place.

Weave as shown in Drawing 5. Start at the line you drew 1 inch up from the bottom of the loom. Pass the shuttle under-over-under-over the warp threads until you reach the other side. Pull the yarn through carefully until there is only a 3-inch-long end sticking out where you started.

For the next row, weave back *under* warp threads wherever you went *over* in the row before, and go *over* wherever you went *under* before.

Continue weaving new rows until you reach the 1-inch line at the top of the loom. Drawing 6.

Cut the warp thread at top right and tie it to the end of the woof thread. Then cut the next warp thread and tie it to these two threads. Now cut the remaining warp threads two at a time, tying each two together as you go. Drawing 7. Repeat at the

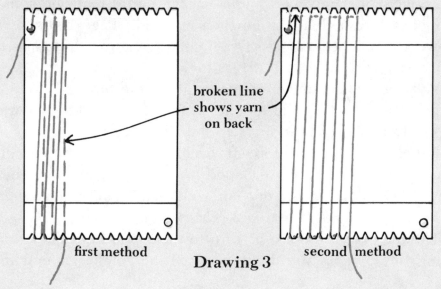

broken line shows yarn on back

first method   **Drawing 3**   second method

44

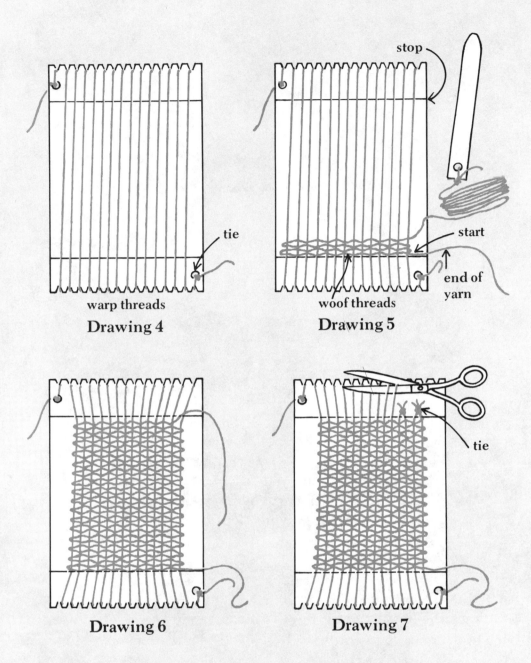

Drawing 4

warp threads

tie

Drawing 5

stop

start

end of
yarn

woof threads

Drawing 6

Drawing 7

tie

bottom. Trim off the fringe and your woven material is finished.

The kind of weave you have just made is called *plain weave.*
Another kind, called *twill weave,* is made by weaving over and
under two warp threads at a time. Try it—the diagonal pattern
may surprise you.

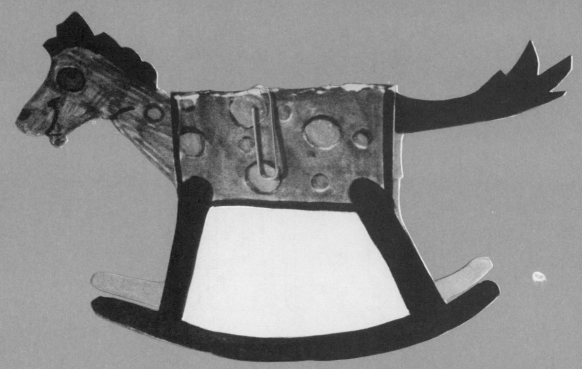

Rocking, Bucking Horse

Materials: tracing paper; masking tape; lightweight cardboard; paper clip. Tools: pencil; scissors; crayons. Optional: carbon paper.

TO MAKE A ROCKING HORSE that will buck like a bronco:

Trace the horse's body and the rockers. See Drawing. Transfer both tracings to cardboard. (Pages 184 and 185 show how.) Cut them out.

Color the horse.

Fold the rocker cutout along the dotted line, and place over the horse's back. Fasten the two pieces with a paper clip as shown in the photograph. Fold the legs outward slightly.

If you move the paper clip forward, your horse will kick up its heels. If you move the clip backward, your horse will buck.

47

Round
Picture Frame

Materials: newspapers to cover work space; crepe paper; paper plates; white glue; old magazines; yarn; adhesive tape. Tools: scissors.

48

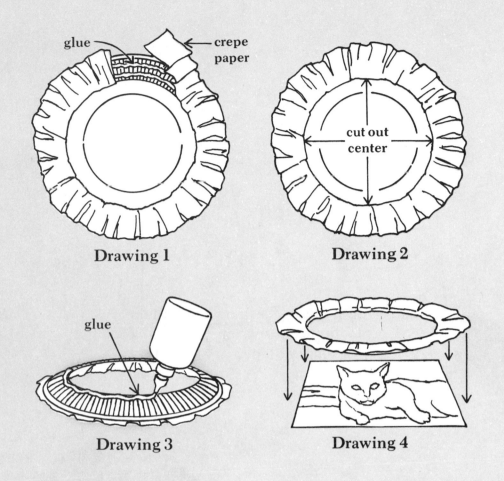

Drawing 1

Drawing 2

Drawing 3

Drawing 4

To show off a picture, give it a round frame.

Cut a piece of crepe paper 2 inches wide and about 24 inches long. Put glue around the border of a paper plate and attach the crepe paper, making folds as you go. See Drawing 1.

Cut out the center of the plate, leaving just the border. Drawing 2.

From a magazine cut out a picture that is slightly larger than the bottom of the paper plate.

Turn the plate over and put glue around the bottom edge. Drawing 3. Turn the plate over again and place it on top of your picture so that the edges of the picture stick to the glue. Drawing 4.

For a hanger use a doubled piece of yarn. Tie a bow at one end. Attach the other end to the frame with adhesive tape.

Sweet Potato Vine

Materials: fresh sweet potato; toothpicks; mason jar; string; transparent tape.

THE SWEET POTATO makes a fine-looking vine to grow indoors. It can grow to a height of six feet or more. To get your vine started, stick six or seven toothpicks in a circle around a sweet potato, near the bigger end. See Drawing 1. Suspend the sweet potato by the toothpicks in a mason jar, with a little bit of the bigger end sticking out. (If your sweet potato is too long for the jar, cut off part of its bottom end.)

Add water until $1/3$ to $1/2$ of the sweet potato is under water. Keep the water at about this level. Drawing 2. Change the water whenever it looks very rusty.

Keep the jar in a dark place—a closet, for instance—until the roots begin to form (probably in about a week). Drawing 3. Then move the jar to a sunny window. Within another two weeks, your sweet potato will form sprouts. Drawing 4.

The vine may grow 12 inches a month. To make it decorate your window, support the vine by strings looped around it and taped to the window frame.

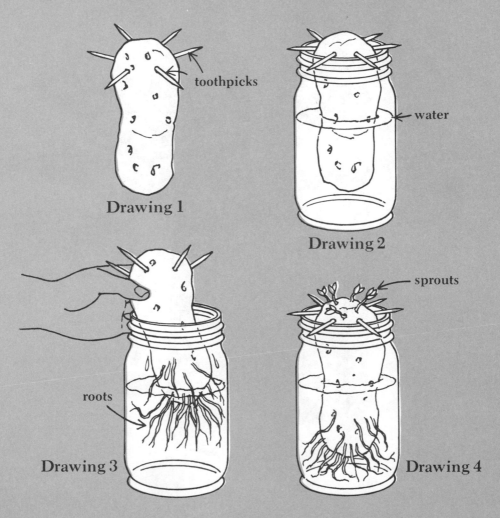

toothpicks

Drawing 1

water

Drawing 2

roots

Drawing 3

sprouts

Drawing 4

Tissue Flower
in a Vase

Materials: five sheets of tissue paper of different colors; pipe cleaners; coffee can, quart milk carton, or large plastic bottle; newspapers. Tools: pencil; scissors; yardstick. Optional: gift-wrapping paper or crepe paper; white glue; enamel paint; thinner; paintbrush.

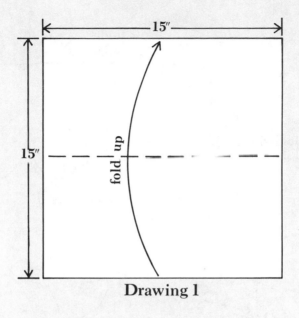

Drawing 1

A broken line shows where to fold.

A colored line shows the last fold made.

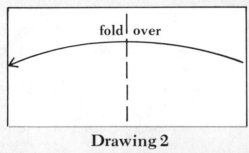

fold over

Drawing 2

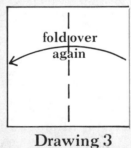

fold over again

Drawing 3

PUT A BIG BRIGHT FLOWER on the breakfast table. Or give it as a special present. Here is how to make it:

Choose five sheets of tissue paper in the colors you want to use for the petals of your flower. Stack the five sheets on top of each other. Measure and draw a square 15 inches by 15 inches on the top sheet. (Page 181 shows how.) Cut out all five squares at the same time.

Pick up the top square only. Fold it three times as shown in Drawings 1, 2, and 3.

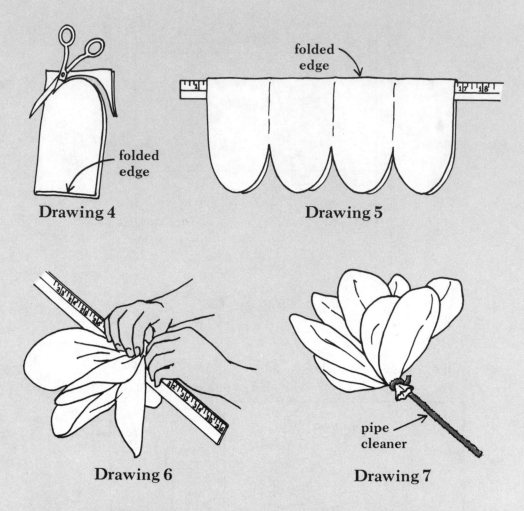

Drawing 4

Drawing 5

Drawing 6

Drawing 7

Starting about halfway up on each side, round off the top with your scissors. Drawing 4.

Open up the tissue paper. Then hang it over a yardstick, with the rounded edges pointing down, as shown in Drawing 5.

Push the tissue together on the yardstick, gathering the part that's pushed together. Drawing 6.

Take hold of the gathered part and wind a pipe cleaner around it to hold it together. Drawing 7.

Do the same with the four other pieces of tissue. When all are finished, twist the five pipe cleaner stems together and wrap another pipe cleaner around them all. Drawing 8.

To make a vase for your flower, first cover your work space with newspapers. Then cover a coffee can or milk carton with gift-wrapping paper or crepe paper, as shown in Drawings 9, 10, and 11. (If you use a milk carton, cut the top off first.)

You can also use a large plastic bottle—an empty bleach bottle or distilled-water bottle—for a vase. Remove the label and, if you wish, paint the bottle with enamel paint.

Drawing 8

Drawing 9

glue

Drawing 10

tuck in

Drawing 11

Paper Bag Puppet

Materials: newspapers to cover work space; brown paper bag; construction paper; white glue. Tools: felt-tip markers or crayons; pencil; scissors. Optional: tracing paper; masking tape; carbon paper.

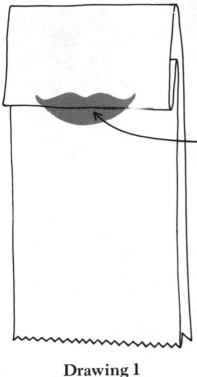

draw mouth
on both
sides of fold

Drawing 1

HAND PUPPETS are often seen on
television shows for children.
They fit on the hand like a mit-
ten. To make a hand puppet for
your own puppet show:

Lay a paper bag flat, with the
bottom fold facing up. Use a
felt-tip pen or crayon to draw a
mouth on the fold. See Drawing
1. Put your hand inside the bag
and see how you can make the
mouth move. Drawing 2.

Flatten the bag again. Cut
hair, hands, and feet out of construction paper. You can copy

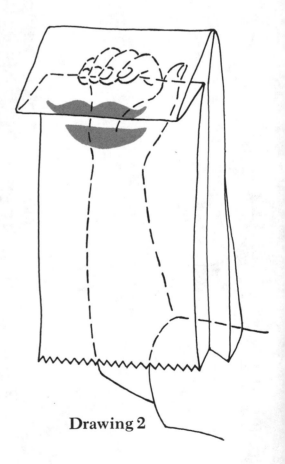

Drawing 2

hair pattern

hand pattern

leg and foot
pattern

Drawing 3

the patterns in Drawing 3, or you can trace them and transfer the tracings to construction paper. (Pages 184 and 185 show how.) Glue the hair, hands, and feet to the bag. Drawing 4.

Draw the eyes, nose, and clothing with felt-tip markers or crayons. Drawing 5.

Your puppet is ready to come alive. Put your hand in the bag and, while you talk or sing, wiggle and bend your fingers to make the puppet's mouth move.

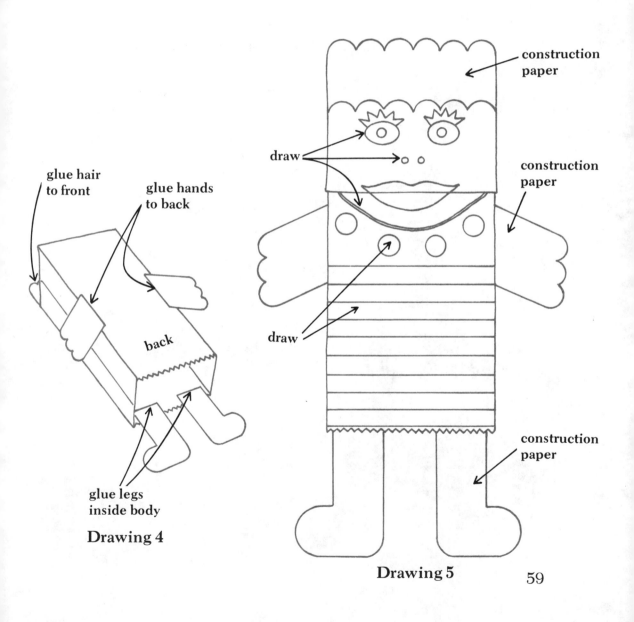

glue hair
to front

glue hands
to back

back

glue legs
inside body

Drawing 4

construction
paper

draw

construction
paper

draw

construction
paper

Drawing 5

Clothespin Theater

Materials: newspapers to cover work space; pictures from old magazines; white glue; clothespins (without springs); sturdy cardboard box; heavy twine. Tools: scissors. Optional: construction paper.

A THEATER IS A SMALL WORLD that is anything you want it to be—a city, a garden, a palace, a ranch. Here is how to make a theater with scenery and clothespin actors:

Cut out colored magazine pictures of people, animals, cars—whatever interests you. Don't cut them out too exactly; leave some background around them. Glue each cut-out on a clothespin, parallel with the slot. See Drawing 1.

Your clothespin actors will clip on to twine strung across the inside of your box theater. For action, you can slide them along on the twine.

To make a stage out of a large cardboard box:

Ask an older person to cut off the top, flaps, and one side. Cut out magazine scenes to make backgrounds for your actors. Glue the scenes around the insides of the box.

Ask an older person to poke holes, from the inside. Run twine through the holes as shown, and knot each piece tightly outside the box. Drawing 2. Now attach your actors to the twine.

To give your stage a finished look, glue construction paper over the stage floor and around the outside of the box.

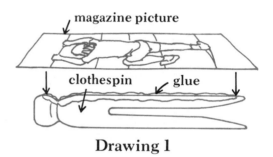

magazine picture

clothespin   glue

Drawing 1

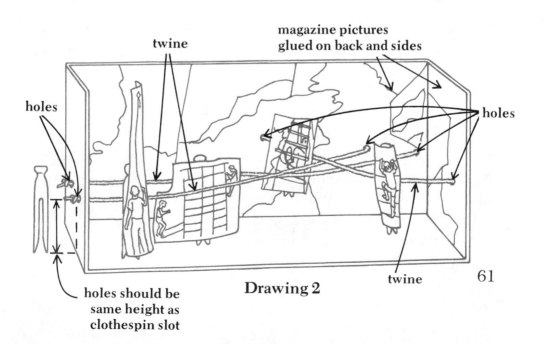

twine

magazine pictures
glued on back and sides

holes

holes

holes

twine

Drawing 2

holes should be
same height as
clothespin slot

61

Folding
Picture Show

Materials: newspapers to cover work space; pictures from old magazines or pictures you have made; medium-weight cardboard; construction paper; white glue; masking tape. Tools: scissors; ruler; pencil.

YOU CAN USE a folding picture show to hold your favorite pictures or to tell a story. Or it can be an ABC book or counting book for a little brother or sister.

To make a folding picture show:

Choose the pictures you want to use for your show. For each picture cut a piece of cardboard about 7 inches wide and about 8 inches long. (Page 180 shows how.) Cut the same number of pieces from colored construction paper. Make each piece the same size as the cardboard pieces. Then paste or glue each colored piece on each cardboard piece. See Drawing 1.

Now paste or glue a picture on the colored side of each piece.

Drawing 2. Then above or below each picture write or print whatever you want to tell about the picture.

Turn the pages over so the pictures face down. Then tape the pages together, side by side, leaving a slight gap between them. Drawing 3. Stand them stretched out on a table or shelf.

To make a folding ABC book:

Use 10 pieces of cardboard and 10 pieces of construction paper. On the first page write or print ABC at the top and use pictures of things whose names start with A, B, and C. On the other nine pages, do the same for DE, FG, HIJ, KLM, NOP, QRS, TUV, WX, and YZ.

To make a counting book:

Use 10 pieces of cardboard and 10 pieces of construction paper. On the first page write 1 at the top and use a picture showing just one thing. On the next page write 2 at the top and show two things. Do the same for pages 3, 4, 5, 6, 7, 8, 9, and 10.

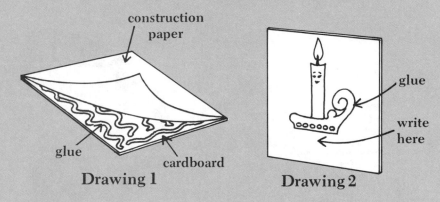

construction paper

glue

cardboard

Drawing 1

glue

write here

Drawing 2

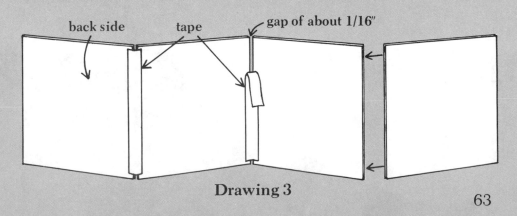

back side   tape   gap of about 1/16"

Drawing 3

63

Paper Cup

Materials: typing paper. Tools: scissors; ruler; pencil.

PAPER FOLDING IS A POPULAR CRAFT in many countries. It is most popular and highly developed in Japan, where it is called origami (pronounced o-ri-GAH-me). For centuries Japanese mothers have taught it to their children.

Originally origami was a ceremonial art, done only for special occasions. The paper had to be square, and only certain folds could be used. Origami specialists taught their students to fold the crane, butterfly, ship, and other classical origami figures. You can start developing your origami talent by making this sturdy cup out of just a piece of paper.

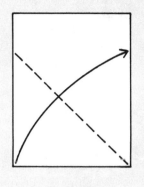

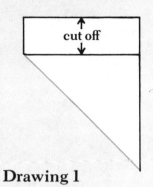

cut off

Drawing 1

A broken line shows where to fold.

A colored line shows the last fold made.

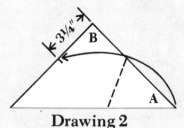

3¼"

B

A

Drawing 2

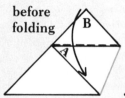

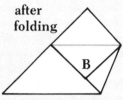

before folding

B

A

after folding

B

Drawing 3

turn paper over

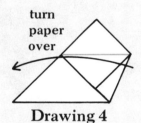

Drawing 4

Fold a bottom corner up to one side. Cut the extra paper off the top, leaving a big folded triangle. See Drawing 1.

With the fold at the bottom, mark the left edge 3¼ inches from the top. Fold point A over to the mark. Drawing 2.

Fold one layer of point B down toward you. Drawing 3.

Turn the paper over as in Drawing 4. Fold corner C over to point D. Drawing 5. Then fold the triangle (B) down toward you. Drawing 6.

Open the cup at the top and it is ready to use.

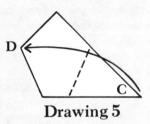

D

C

Drawing 5

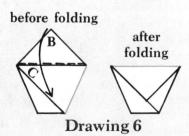

before folding

B

C

after folding

Drawing 6

65

Wall Pocket

Materials: newspapers to cover work space; two paper plates; picture from an old magazine; yarn or cord; white glue; shellac and thinner. Tools: scissors; pencil; ruler; paintbrush. Optional: metal paper fasteners.

66

USE THIS WALL POCKET to store pencils and notepad, trading cards, secret treasures, or a week's supply of gum.

Cut a paper plate in half. Discard one half. Place the other half over a second plate, with the hollow sides of the plates facing each other, to form a pocket. See Drawing 1.

With a pencil, punch holes about 1 inch apart through both paper plate rims. Put paper fasteners in the holes. (If you do not have fasteners, you can lace the two rims together with yarn or cord later, after you have put on shellac.) Now punch two holes side by side in the rim of the whole plate, at the top. Drawing 2.

Cut out a picture from an old magazine and glue it to the half plate.

Shellac the outside of the wall pocket and let it dry over night. (The shellac will make the wall pocket easy to clean with a damp cloth.) Clean your brush in thinner.

For a hanger, use a piece of yarn or cord. Thread it through the two holes at the top and tie the ends.

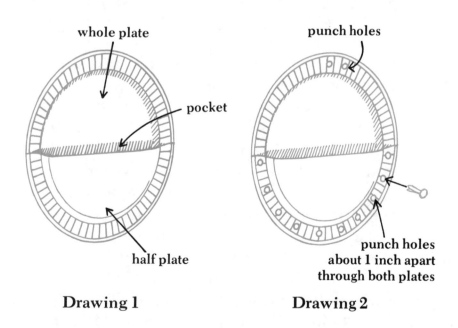

Drawing 1   **Drawing 2**

Jack-in-the-Box

Materials: newspapers to cover work space; typing paper; transparent tape; white glue; medium-weight cardboard. Tools: ruler; pencil; scissors; nail file.

A TOY LIKED BY CHILDREN of many countries for many years is the jack-in-the-box. Here is how to make one for yourself:

Cut eight strips of paper 1 inch wide and 11 inches long. (Page 180 shows how.) Tape four of them together, end to end. Mark this new strip "A." Tape the other four strips together. Mark this new strip "B." See Drawing 1.

Lay the end of strip A across strip B, one inch from the end of B. Drawing 2. Fold that inch over onto strip A. Drawing 3.

Now fold strip A up over strip B. Drawing 4.

Fold strip B back over strip A, A down over B, B over A, and so on to the ends. Drawings 5, 6, and 7. There should be an extra inch of A left over. Fold it around behind B, tucking it in. Drawing 8.

To make Jack's head, cut a piece of paper 1 inch by 2 inches. Fold back the bottom half. Draw a funny face on the top half. Drawing 9. Then glue the bottom half to one end of the folded strips. Drawing 10.

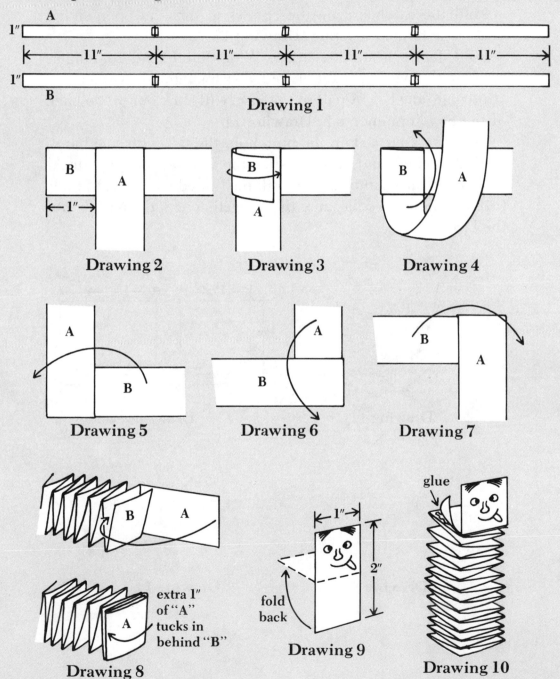

To make a base, cut a piece of cardboard 2½ inches long and 1⅜ inches wide. Glue the bottom of the folded strips to one end of this piece of cardboard. Drawing 11.

For Jack's box, cut a piece of cardboard 4 inches long and 1½ inches wide. Measure off the dimensions shown in Drawing 12, mark the lines, and, with a nail file, scratch them so they dent the cardboard.

Fold the cardboard on the creases to form an open-ended box. Tape to hold together. Drawing 13.

Fold Jack's head down flat. With thumb and forefinger, squeeze the whole packet of folded strips tightly together and slip it into the box. A part of the base will stick out of the back of the box, forming a tab. Drawing 14.

To work your jack-in-the-box, hold the tab with one hand. With the other hand, quickly slide the box out. Up pops Jack!

To make Jack jump farther, pull the folded strips out to their full length before squeezing them together to fit them back into the box.

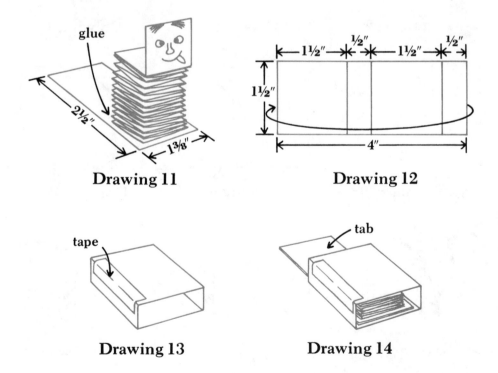

Drawing 11

Drawing 12

Drawing 13

Drawing 14

Maracas

Materials: newspapers to cover work space; two round balloons; white glue; 24 dried beans or small pebbles; two cardboard tubes; masking tape; paint; crepe paper. Tools: jar; ruler; scissors; measuring cup; foil pan; pin; paintbrush.

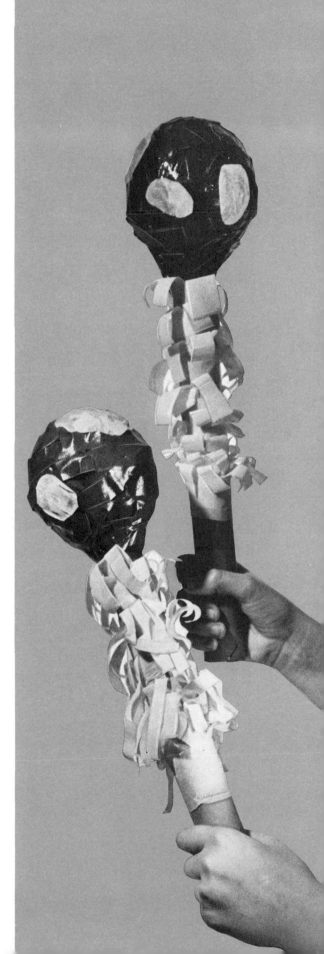

MARACAS (say "mah-*rock*-ahs") are rattles used in playing Latin American music. They make a swishy sound. The maracas player shakes a maraca with each hand to mark the rhythm of the music. The Indians of South America, the first people to use maracas, make theirs out of gourds. Here is how to make yours:

Blow up two balloons to the size of a grapefruit. Tie the end of each.

Place one of the balloons in

71

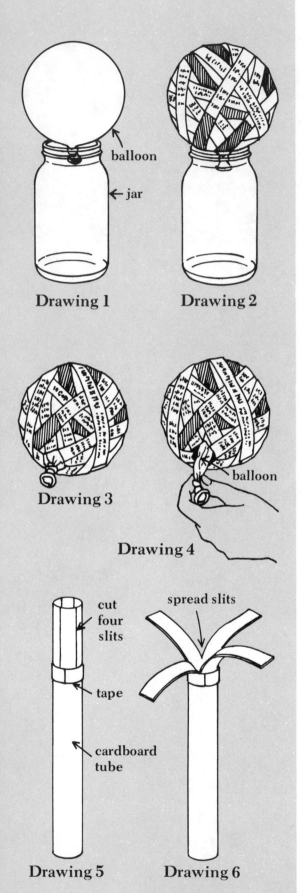

Drawing 1

balloon

jar

Drawing 2

Drawing 3

Drawing 4

balloon

cut
four
slits

spread slits

tape

cardboard
tube

Drawing 5

Drawing 6

the mouth of a jar. See Drawing 1.

Cut strips of newspaper about 6 inches long by 1/2 inch wide. (Save time by cutting triple layers.)

In a foil pan, mix equal amounts of white glue and water—about 1/2 cup of each. Dip the newspaper strips in this mixture and apply the wet strips to the balloon, criss-crossing them. Drawing 2. Use about five layers, to make the maraca strong. Make sure that no part of the balloon shows through except at the very bottom. Drawing 3.

Do the same with the second balloon. Let both balloons dry overnight.

Hold each balloon in turn by the tied end and burst it with a pin. When the balloon has gotten small enough, pull it out by the tied end. Drawing 4.

Insert 12 beans or pebbles through the hole in each maraca and tape the hole closed.

To make handles, use a cardboard tube for each maraca. A tube from gift-wrapping paper is best, but you can use a paper towel tube instead.

72

Cut four parallel slits into the end of each tube, running lengthwise. Make each slit about 3 inches long. Circle the tubes with tape just below the slits to keep them from splitting farther. Drawing 5.

Spread the slit pieces apart. Drawing 6. Fit the maracas onto the slit pieces and tape the slit pieces firmly to the maracas. Drawings 7 and 8.

Paint the maracas and let dry overnight.

To decorate the handles, cut two strips of crepe paper about 3 inches wide and 14 inches long. Cut 1½-inch slits all along the edge of each strip, about ¼ inch apart. This will make a fringe.

Glue the uncut edge of one strip to the handle of one of the maracas, starting just below the maraca. Wind and glue the strip around the handle toward the bottom end. Drawing 9. Repeat with the other handle.

Cut out several crepe paper circles and glue them on the maracas.

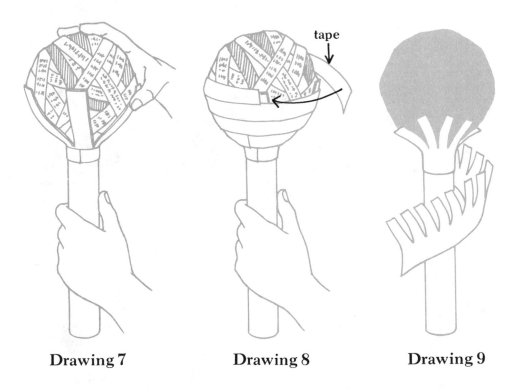

Drawing 7   **Drawing 8**   **Drawing 9**

Shadow Camera

Materials: white paper; masking tape; colored paper; white glue. Tools: unshaded electric light or gooseneck lamp; pencil; scissors.

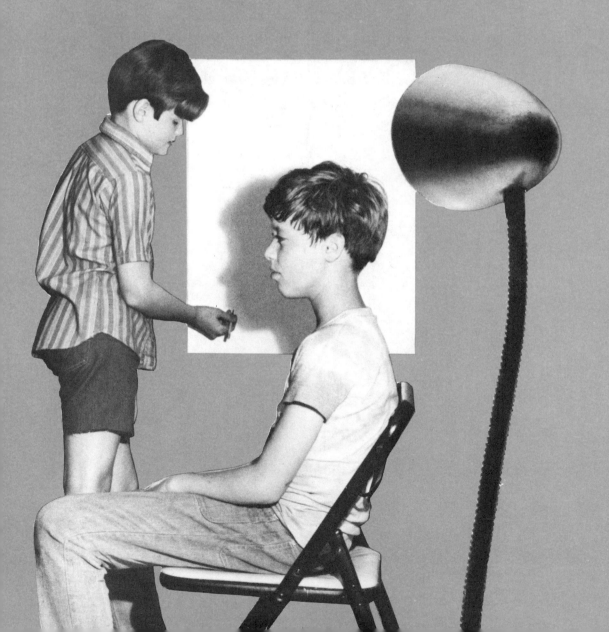

HERE'S A WAY to catch a shadow:

Tape a large piece of white paper to a door or paneled wall. Place an unshaded electric light so it will shine on the paper. You can also use a gooseneck lamp, like the one in the photograph. Have one of your friends sit still in front of the light so that his shadow can be seen on the paper. Draw around the edge of the shadow with a pencil. Cut the picture out and glue it on a piece of colored paper.

You can make a large shadow picture by placing the light close to your model, and a small one by placing the light far away.

Paper Glider

Materials: typing paper or notebook paper; paper clips.

SOME PILOTS CAN FLY their gliders for hundreds of miles by catching the winds the right way. Their gliders are made out of wood or light metal. Test your skill with this paper glider. Here is how to make it:

Fold a sheet of paper in half the long way. See Drawing 1.

Fold one corner out and back so that it touches the bottom edge. Drawing 2.

Do the same with the opposite corner—fold it back so that it touches the bottom on the opposite side. Drawing 3.

Make the wings by folding in half down the entire length of both sides of the glider. Drawing 4.

Open the wings so they point slightly upward. Fasten one or two paper clips to the bottom of the glider, near the front. Drawing 5.

The weight of the paper clips will help your glider fly farther. If you want a longer flight, try adding more paper clips or moving the clips until they are in just the right spot.

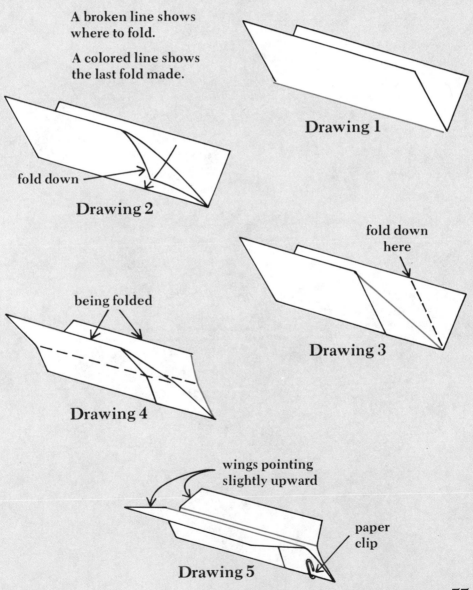

A broken line shows where to fold.

A colored line shows the last fold made.

Drawing 1

fold down

Drawing 2

being folded

Drawing 4

fold down here

Drawing 3

wings pointing slightly upward

paper clip

Drawing 5

Paper Beads

Materials: typing paper; lightweight cardboard; transparent tape; strong thread; pictures from old magazines. Tools: ruler; pencil; scissors; needle; round toothpick.

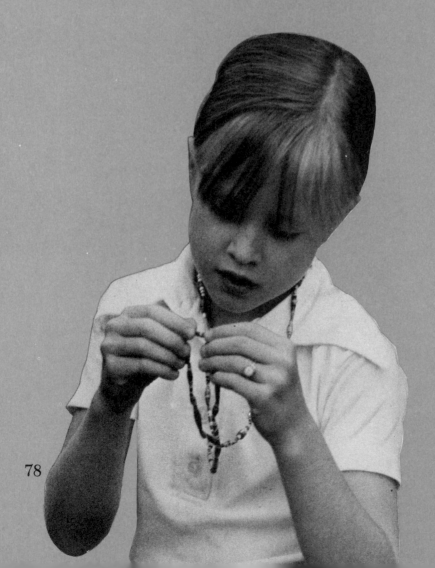

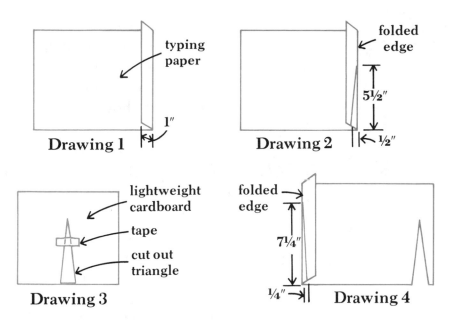

typing paper

Drawing 1   1″

folded edge

5½″   ½″

Drawing 2

lightweight cardboard

tape

cut out triangle

Drawing 3

folded edge

7¼″

¼″   Drawing 4

EACH OF THESE MANY-COLORED BEADS will surprise you—because each is different. String them together to make one-of-a-kind necklaces and bracelets. To fill your jewelry box or surprise someone:

Fold up 1 inch at the bottom of a sheet of typing paper. See Drawing 1.

On the folded part, mark off ½ inch on the short edge and 5½ inches on the long edge, as shown in Drawing 2. Draw a line joining the two marks.

Cut out along the pencil line. Unfold. This triangle will be the pattern for one set of beads. To make the pattern easier to use, tape it to a piece of lightweight cardboard and cut out the cardboard. Drawing 3.

Now fold up 1 inch at the other end of the sheet of paper. On the folded part, mark off ¼ inch on the short edge and 7¼ inches on the long edge. Join the two marks, cut out along the line, and unfold. Drawing 4. This triangle will be the pattern for a second set of beads. Tape it to a piece of cardboard and cut out.

For a necklace, put a length of thread around your neck and cut the thread off when it is as long as you want your necklace to be. Then thread it through a needle.

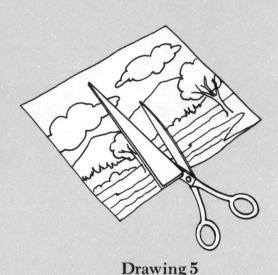

Drawing 5

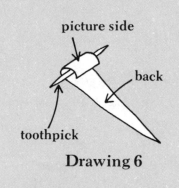

picture side

back

toothpick

Drawing 6

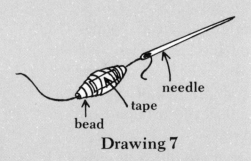

needle

tape

bead

Drawing 7

Pick some colorful pictures in an old magazine. Magazines with glossy paper are best. What the pictures show doesn't matter.

Put one of your triangle patterns on a picture, draw around it, and cut the triangle out. Drawing 5.

Lay a round toothpick on the back side of the picture triangle, across the wide end. Roll the triangle up around the toothpick. Drawing 6. Roll straight so that the two sides taper evenly. This makes a bead.

Tape the loose end to keep the bead from unrolling. Remove the toothpick and run the needle through the hole to thread the bead. Drawing 7.

Repeat, using the other triangle pattern, to make a differently shaped bead. Keep changing the triangle patterns until your necklace is completely threaded with beads. Then tie the ends together.

You can make differently shaped beads by changing the size of the triangle pattern. Experiment until you find some new shapes you like.

You can make bracelets instead of necklaces by stringing the beads on shorter threads.

80

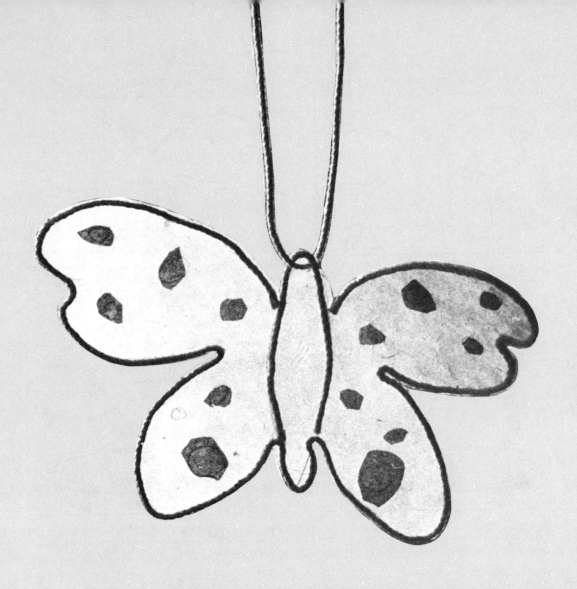

Stained-Glass Window Ornament

Materials: newspapers to cover work space; pictures from old magazines; white glue; light-weight cardboard; tissue paper or crepe paper; twine; transparent tape. Tools: pencil; scissors; foil pan; plastic straw or stick.

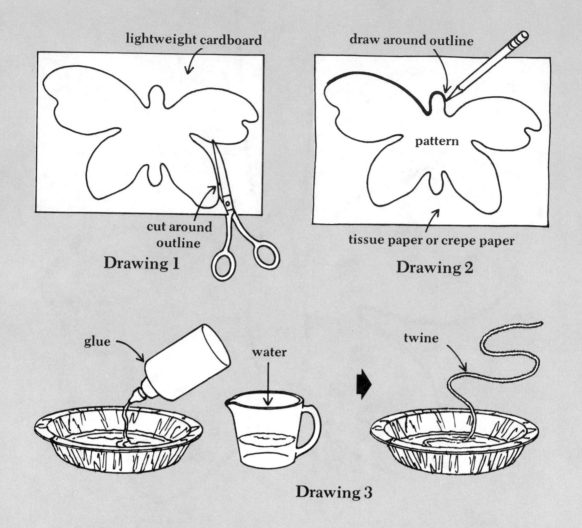

lightweight cardboard

cut around
outline

Drawing 1

draw around outline

pattern

tissue paper or crepe paper

Drawing 2

glue

water

twine

Drawing 3

STAINED GLASS IS THE COLORED GLASS you may have seen in church windows. Light shining through it makes the colors glow.

This ornament will glow like stained glass if you hang it in a sunny window. Here is how to make it:

Find a picture about 4 inches high in an old magazine and cut it out. Then glue the picture to lightweight cardboard for a pattern. Or you can draw your own pattern on cardboard.

Cut out the cardboard pattern. See Drawing 1. Place the pattern on a piece of colored tissue paper or crepe paper. Draw around the outline. Drawing 2.

Mix some glue and water in a foil pan—about two table-

82

spoons of each. (Don't squeeze glue into a spoon. Ask an older person for help in guessing how much glue to squeeze out.) Stir the mixture with a straw or a stick.

Measure out enough twine to go all the way around the ornament's outline. Dip the twine in the glue-water mixture. Drawing 3.

Lay the wet twine on the ornament's outline, going all the way around. Drawing 4. Cut off any twine left over.

You can decorate your ornament by gluing on pieces of tissue paper or crepe paper. Or you can glue on additional twine. Drawing 5.

When the twine is dry, cut out the ornament outside of the twine outline. Punch a hole with your pencil at the top. Put a piece of twine through the hole for a hanger.

Tape the hanger to a bright window with transparent tape, so that the light shows through.

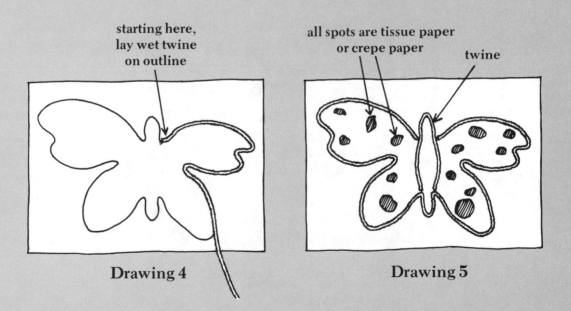

starting here, lay wet twine on outline

all spots are tissue paper or crepe paper

twine

Drawing 4

Drawing 5

Yarn
Holder

Materials: newspapers to cover
work space; oatmeal or cornmeal
box; gift-wrapping paper; white
glue; yarn; paper clips. Tools: scissors; pencil; ruler; thumbtack.

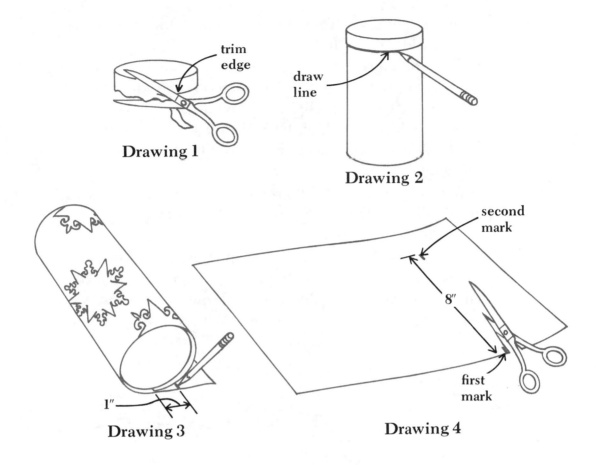

Drawing 1

trim edge

Drawing 2

draw line

Drawing 3

1"

Drawing 4

second mark

8"

first mark

THIS YARN HOLDER is for someone who loves to knit. It keeps the ball of yarn from escaping or tangling as it's used. To please your favorite yarn-user:

Remove the cover from a round oatmeal or cornmeal box. Trim any extra paper off the bottom edge of the cover, to make it even. See Drawing 1.

Replace the cover and draw a line around the box along the bottom edge of the cover. Drawing 2. Remove the cover again.

Place the box on the back of a piece of gift-wrapping paper. Roll the paper around the box. Let the paper overlap about 1 inch, and mark that point at the edge of the paper. Drawing 3.

Unroll the paper. Mark a point about 8 inches in and cut straight across the paper from the first pencil mark to the second. Drawing 4.

Now measure the box, from the pencil line near the top to the bottom, and add ¹/₂ inch to this measurement. Drawing 5.

Mark that measurement along the cut line and along the opposite edge of the paper. Cut from one mark to the other to get the strip of paper you will use. Drawing 6.

Draw a straight line ¹/₂ inch from the edge on the long side. Then mark off one-inch spaces and cut out to form notches and tabs. Drawing 7.

Glue the strip to the box, with the unnotched edge even with the pencil line near the top. Drawing 8. Fold the tabs over the bottom of the box and glue them down.

Draw a circle on the gift-wrapping paper, using the bottom of the box as a guide. Now draw another circle around the first one. The second circle should be ¹/₂ inch outside the first one. (It can be rough because it won't show.) Draw V-shaped lines

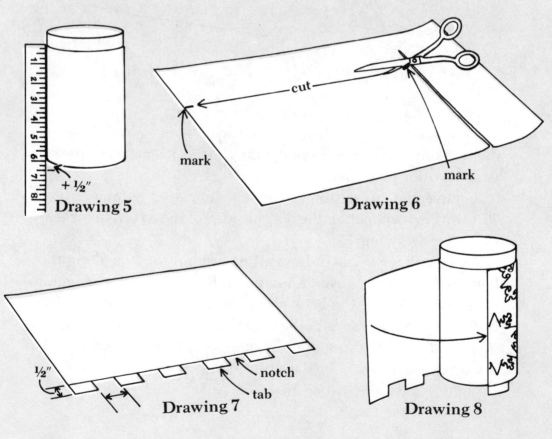

Drawing 5

Drawing 6

Drawing 7

Drawing 8

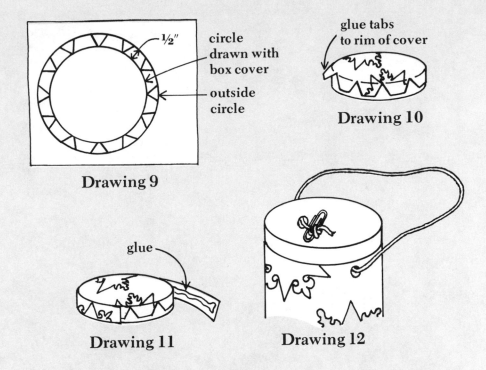

1/2"

circle drawn with box cover

outside circle

Drawing 9

glue tabs to rim of cover

Drawing 10

glue

Drawing 11

Drawing 12

between the two circles. Drawing 9. Cut out the larger circle and then cut along the V-shaped lines to form tabs. Center this piece on the cover and glue it. Fold the tabs down around the rim and glue them. Drawing 10.

Now cut out a strip of gift-wrapping paper for the cover's rim. It should be the same width as the rim and the same length as the paper used to cover the box. Glue the strip onto the rim to hide the tabs. Drawing 11.

Draw another circle on gift-wrapping paper, using the bottom of the box as a guide. Cut it out and glue to the bottom of the box. (This circle does not need notches.)

Using a thumbtack, punch two holes on opposite sides of the box about 2 inches down from the top. Make the holes bigger with a pencil. Thread the ends of a 12-inch piece of yarn through the holes from the outside. Knot the ends around paper clips so the handle won't pull out. Drawing 12.

Using a thumbtack, punch a hole in the center of the cover. Use a pencil to make it big enough for yarn to pass through easily.

Crowns

Materials: newspapers to cover work space; string; lightweight cardboard; metallic (shiny) gift-wrapping paper; white glue; glitter and sequins for large crown; rickrack (zigzag cloth trim) for small crown; transparent tape. Tools: scissors; ruler; pencil; dinner plate for large crown; soup can for small crown.

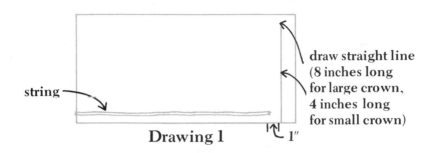

draw straight line
(8 inches long
for large crown,
4 inches long
for small crown)

string

Drawing 1   1"

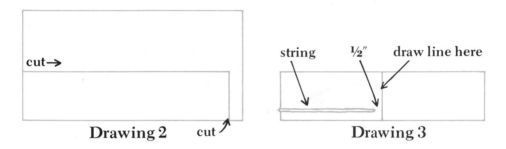

cut→

Drawing 2   cut↗

string   ½"   draw line here

Drawing 3

ROYAL CROWNS ARE SET with the finest jewels in the world. Famous crowns like those of England's kings and queens glitter with diamonds, rubies, gold, and silver. To crown yourself king or queen:

Measure the size of your head by tying a string around it at the forehead. Take the string off your head and cut it at the knot. Stretch the string along the bottom edge of a piece of cardboard. One inch past the end of the string, draw a line across the cardboard as shown in Drawing 1. For the large crown, make this line 8 inches long; for the small crown, 4 inches long.

From the tip of the first line draw a second line to the opposite edge of the cardboard, forming a rectangle. Cut out the rectangle. Drawing 2.

Fold the string over and cut it in half. Stretch out one piece on the cardboard as shown in Drawing 3. Draw a line across the cardboard ½ inch past the end of this string. This line marks the center of the cardboard.

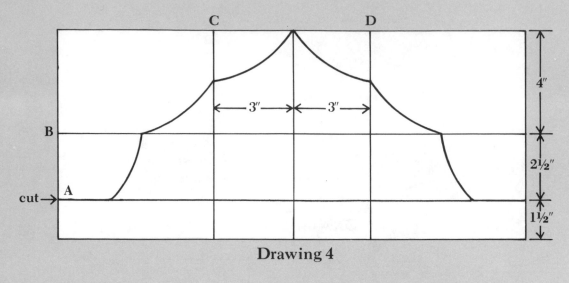

Drawing 4

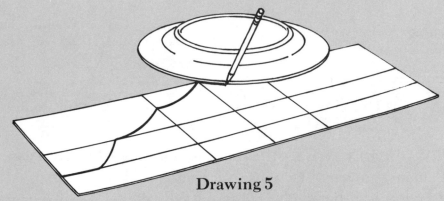

Drawing 5

For the large crown, do these things:

Draw lines A, B, C, and D as shown in Drawing 4.

Then, draw curved lines as shown on the drawing. (Use a dinner plate as a guide for the curves. Drawing 5.) Cut out along the curved lines.

Place the cardboard on the back of a piece of shiny wrapping paper. Trace the crown's outline. Cut out the paper and glue it to the cardboard.

Squeeze out glue to form a band along the top and bottom on the front of the crown. Sprinkle with glitter. (Along the bottom you may want to add a decorative ribbon instead.) To add jewels, squeeze out glue to make a large oval and several small circles, and sprinkle with sequins. Drawing 6.

When the glue is dry, overlap the crown's ends by one inch and tape or staple together. Drawing 7.

90

For the small crown, do these things:

Draw lines A, B, and C as shown in Drawing 8.

Draw curved lines as shown in Drawing 9. (Use a soup can as a guide for the curves.) Cut out along the curved lines.

Place the cardboard on the back of a piece of shiny wrapping paper. Trace the crown's outline. Cut out the paper and glue it to the cardboard. Glue rickrack to the bottom edge of the crown.

Overlap the crown's ends at the back by one inch and tape together.

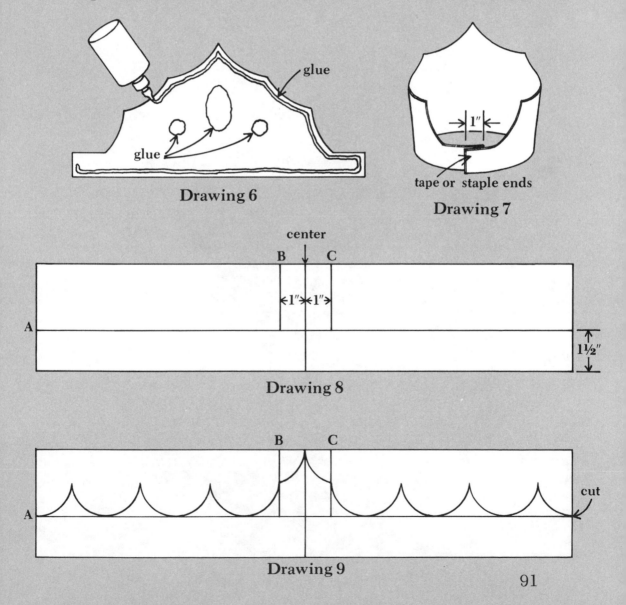

Drawing 6

Drawing 7

Drawing 8

Drawing 9

91

Stars

Materials: typing paper. Tools: pencil; ruler; scissors.

Can you cut out a perfect star? Try these ways of making stars. Then ask your friends to guess how you did it.

For a six-pointed star, cut out a square measuring about 8 inches on each side. (Page 181 shows how.)

Fold the square in half. See Drawing 1.

Fold in half again, to form a square. Drawing 2.

Fold the square in half. Drawing 3. Now unfold so that you have a rectangle again. Drawing 4.

As shown in Drawing 5, fold corner A up to make a diagonal fold running from the top of crease B to the bottom of crease C.

Now fold the other part up so that side D rests along side E. Drawing 6.

Your paper should now look like Drawing 7.

Turn the paper over and fold in half as shown. Drawing 8.

Cut as shown in Drawing 9. Unfold to find your star.

SIX-POINTED STAR

A broken line shows where to fold. A gray line shows a crease. A colored line shows the last fold made.

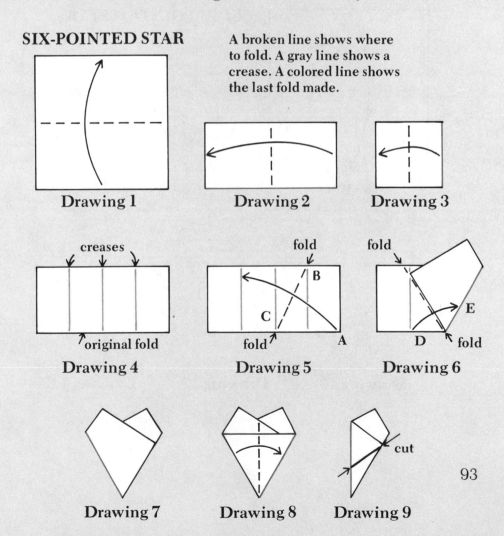

Drawing 1

Drawing 2

Drawing 3

creases

original fold

Drawing 4

fold

B

C

fold

A

Drawing 5

fold

fold

E

D

fold

Drawing 6

Drawing 7

Drawing 8

cut

Drawing 9

93

For a five-pointed star, cut a square of paper 3 inches by 3 inches or larger. Then fold it in half. Drawing 10.

With the fold at the top, bring the right-hand top corner over to point A on the left-hand side. (Point A is about ⅓ of the way up the side.) Fold. Drawing 11.

Your paper will look like Drawing 12.

Now fold the corner at the right over to point A as shown in Drawing 12. Your paper will look like Drawing 13.

Now fold the left upper corner down as far as it will go as shown in Drawing 13. Your paper will look like Drawing 14.

Cut across all the folds at an angle, as shown in Drawing 14. Then unfold the top part to find your five-pointed star.

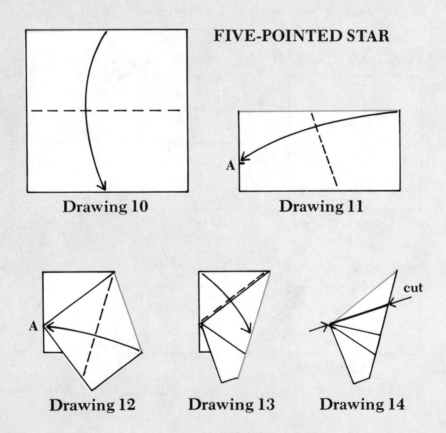

FIVE-POINTED STAR

Drawing 10   Drawing 11

Drawing 12   Drawing 13   Drawing 14

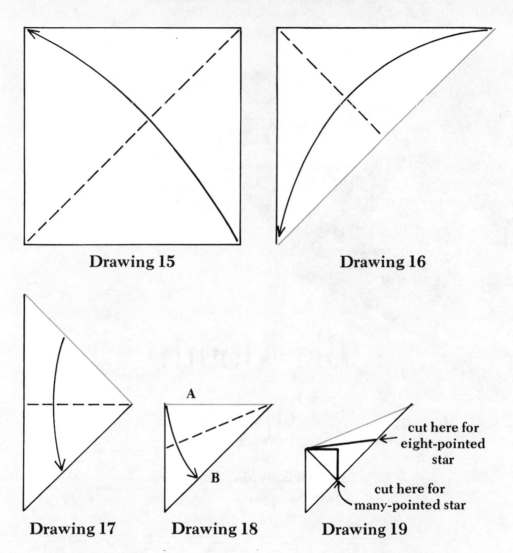

Drawing 15   Drawing 16

A

B

Drawing 17   Drawing 18   Drawing 19

cut here for
eight-pointed
star

cut here for
many-pointed star

For a many-pointed star, cut out a square measuring about 8 inches on each side. Fold the paper diagonally. Drawing 15.

Fold again, as in Drawing 16, and again, as in Drawing 17. Now fold so that side A lines up with side B. Drawing 18.

For an eight-pointed star, cut a straight line as shown in Drawing 19. For a many-pointed star, cut an upside-down "L" as shown in Drawing 19.

Big-Mouth
Puppet

**Materials: typing paper or
notebook paper.**

START PRACTICING your squawks and growls! Big-Mouth
Puppet will need some sound effects when he snaps at a nearby
finger.

First, fold a sheet of paper in half. See Drawing 1.

With the fold at the bottom, fold the top leaf in half. Fold
outward. Drawing 2.

Fold the bottom leaf in half. Fold outward. Drawing 3.

Turn the paper over so that the fold is at the top. Turn up

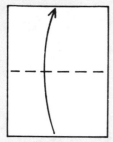

A broken line shows where to fold.
A colored line shows the last fold made.

Drawing 1

bottom leaf

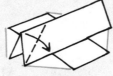

top
leaf

Drawing 2

bottom leaf

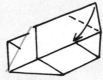

Drawing 3

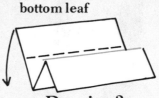

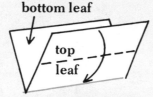

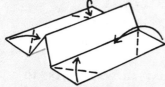

Drawing 4

Drawing 5

Drawing 6

Drawing 7

each of the four bottom corners. Drawing 4.

Fold down the two top corners. Drawings 5 and 6.

Then fold up the two sides.
Drawing 7.

Turn over and make a small
tear across the two long edges,
about in the middle. Now fold
each side down at the tear.
Drawings 8 and 9.

Spread apart as in Drawing
10. Then squeeze together as
in Drawing 11.

You now have a Big-Mouth
Puppet. He's a bird! He's a
dragon! He's a hat! (A hat?
Yes—if you use a sheet of
newspaper folded the same
way it will make a paper hat
big enough to wear.)

tear,
then fold

Drawing 8

torn edges

Drawing 9

spread   apart

Drawing 10

squeeze
at
arrows

Drawing 11

97

Pencil or Paintbrush Holder

Materials: newspapers to cover work space; round oatmeal or cornmeal box; plastic berry basket; white glue; poster paint. **Tools:** can, jar, or lid slightly smaller across than the round box; pencil; scissors; ruler; paintbrush. **Optional:** crayon or felt-tip marker; construction paper.

CORRAL YOUR PENCILS AND PAINTBRUSHES in this holder. For a party, stand straws or lollipops in it. To make one:

Take the cover off an oatmeal or cornmeal box. Using a can (or jar or lid) as a pattern, draw a circle on the cover. See Drawing 1. Cut along the circle, cutting out the center of the cover. Drawing 2.

Now cut off the bottom of a berry basket. Use the rim of the cover as a pattern to cut the bottom of the berry basket into a circle. Make sure the circle will fit inside the rim. Drawing 3. Glue the circle inside the rim. Drawing 4.

Draw a line around the box 4 inches from the bottom. One

way to do this is to measure off 4 inches, put your pencil against the box at this point, and turn the box to draw the line. Drawing 5. Cut along this line.

Put the cover on the box and paint the outside of the box and the cover with poster paint. Clean your paintbrush in water.

After the paint is dry, glue on decorations.

For a smiling-face decoration, draw a head, eyes, and mouth on construction paper with crayon or felt-tip marker. Drawing 6. Make several faces, cut them out, and glue them on.

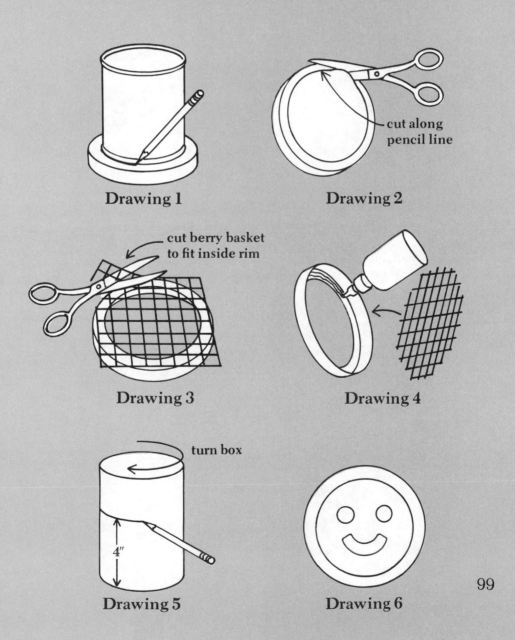

Drawing 1

Drawing 2

cut along
pencil line

cut berry basket
to fit inside rim

Drawing 3

Drawing 4

turn box

4"

Drawing 5

Drawing 6

99

Box Train

Materials: three or more shoe boxes; twine; four or more small sticks. Tools: thumbtack; pencil; scissors; juice glass or small can; black crayon. Optional: poster paint; paintbrush.

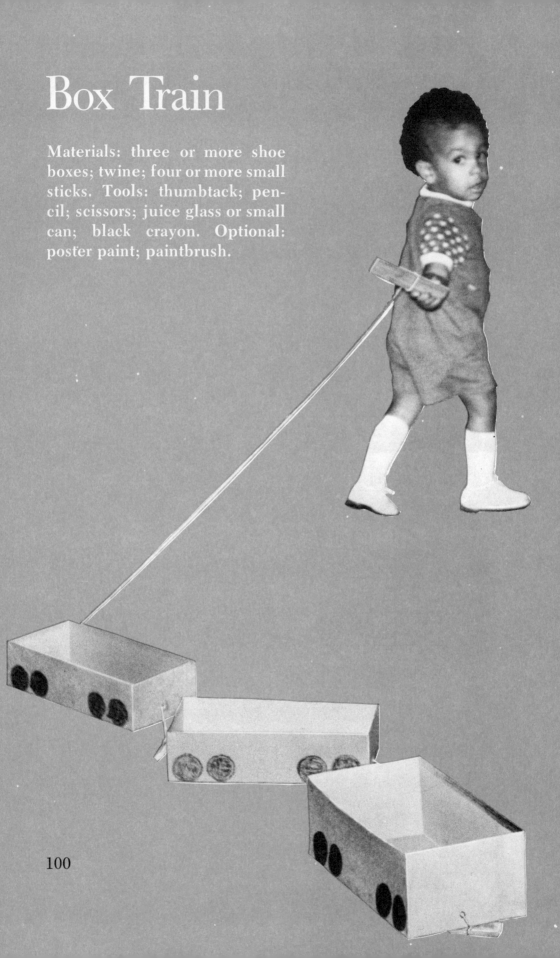

100

Do you need a freight train to carry your toys? A passenger train to carry your dolls? You will be the engine for this train!

You can use the boxes just as they are or you can paint the outsides. See Drawing 1.

With a thumbtack punch holes through both ends of each box, about in the middle, near the bottom. Drawing 2. Make the holes larger by pushing a pencil through each. Drawing 3.

Cut a piece of twine about 2 yards long. Tie a stick to one end of the twine. Drawing 4.

Pass the twine through the holes of the first box. Pull until the stick is up against the end of the box. Tie a second stick to the twine in front of the first box. Leave enough room so the boxes will not bump—at least 6 inches. Drawing 5.

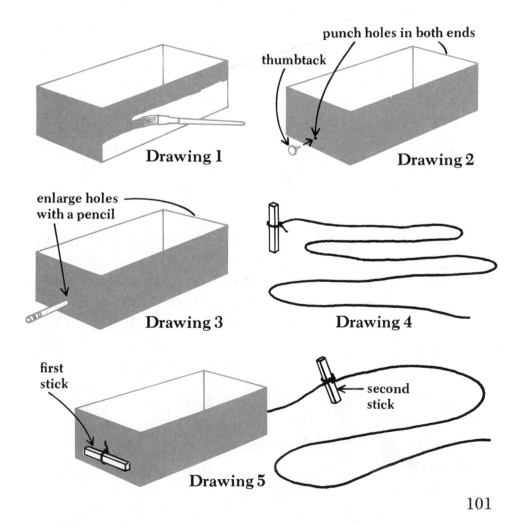

thumbtack

punch holes in both ends

Drawing 1

Drawing 2

enlarge holes
with a pencil

Drawing 3

Drawing 4

first
stick

second
stick

Drawing 5

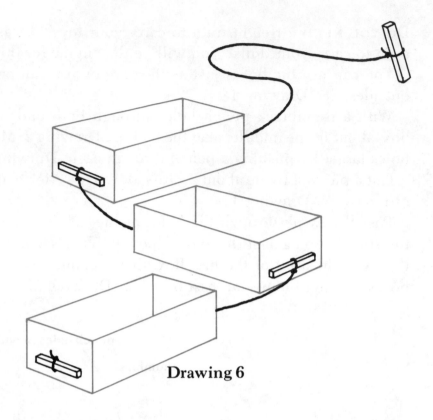

Drawing 6

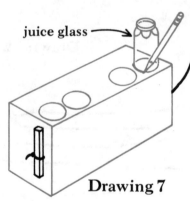

juice glass →

Drawing 7

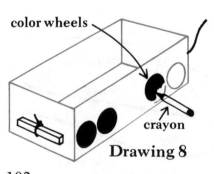

color wheels

crayon

Drawing 8

Pass the twine through the second box and tie another stick ahead of that box. Do the same for any other boxes you want to add to your train. Then tie a stick to the loose end of the twine for a handle. Drawing 6. Using a juice glass or small can as a guide, draw wheels on the boxes. Drawing 7. Color the wheels. Drawing 8. Load the boxes with toys or dolls and away you go.

Costume Patterns

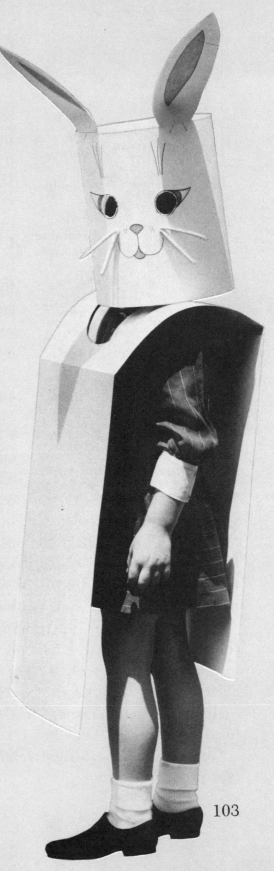

Materials: lightweight cardboard (two pieces of lightweight poster board measuring 22 by 28 inches will work best); masking tape. Tools: scissors; ruler; pencil; dinner plate about 9 inches across.

NEED A COSTUME? Here's a way to make almost any kind you want—for Halloween, for parties, for a play, or just for fun:

Cut a large piece of cardboard to measure 22 inches by 28 inches. Then cut it in half the long way to get two pieces each measuring 14 inches by 22 inches. These two pieces are the front and back.

Cut another piece of cardboard to measure 14 inches by 12 inches. This is the shoulder piece. Draw a circle about 9 inches across in the middle of the shoulder piece. (Use a din-

103

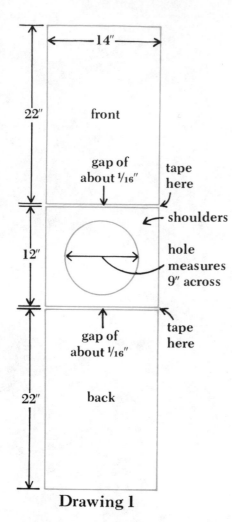

Drawing 1

ner plate as a guide.) Cut along the circle to make a hole for your head.

With the three pieces not quite touching, tape the shoulder piece to the front and back pieces. Use tape on both sides. Drawing 1.

Cut out a piece of cardboard to measure 11 inches by 28 inches for the mask. Curve the cardboard so the edges overlap, forming a cylinder. Tape the cardboard together, using a short piece of tape at the top and bottom. Drawing 2.

Put the mask over your head and feel where your eyes are. Mark these places with a pencil. Untape the mask and cut out eyeholes. The next step depends on what kind of a costume you want to make.

To make a rabbit costume you will need the materials listed at the beginning to make the basic costume. You will also need lightweight white cardboard for the ears, two pipe cleaners, pink crayon, black felt-tip marker, stapler, white glue, and newspapers to cover your work space.

Follow the general instructions given earlier. With a black felt-tip marker, draw a face on the mask. Color the nose and tongue pink. Drawing 3. Then roll the mask back into a cylinder and staple shut.

Bend two pipe cleaners in the middle and glue beside the nose for whiskers. Drawing 4.

Cut two ears from lightweight cardboard. Color the inner part pink. Drawing 5.

Cut a small notch at the base of each ear. Drawing 6. Staple the edges of each notch together. Drawing 7. Then staple the ears to the mask. Drawing 8.

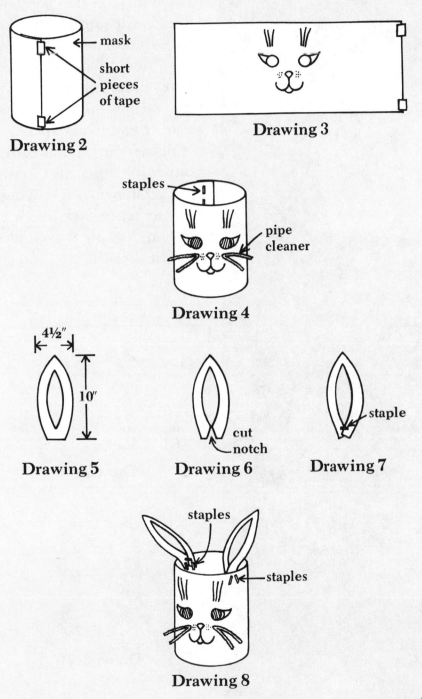

Drawing 2

Drawing 3

Drawing 4

Drawing 5

Drawing 6

Drawing 7

Drawing 8

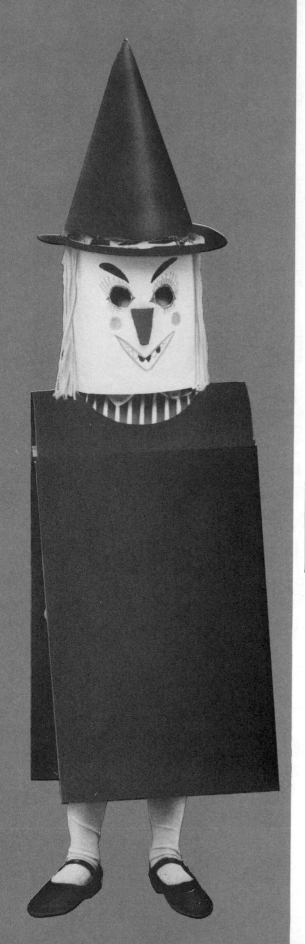

To make a witch costume you will need the materials listed at the beginning for the basic costume. Use black cardboard for the body and white cardboard for the face. You will also need yarn (black or yellow), felt-tip markers, white glue, stapler, thumbtack, string, and newspapers to cover your work space.

Follow the general instructions given earlier. Draw a face as shown in Drawing 9. Roll the mask back into a cylinder and staple it shut along the seam at the top and bottom.

draw with
felt-tip marker

Drawing 9

Drawing 10

106

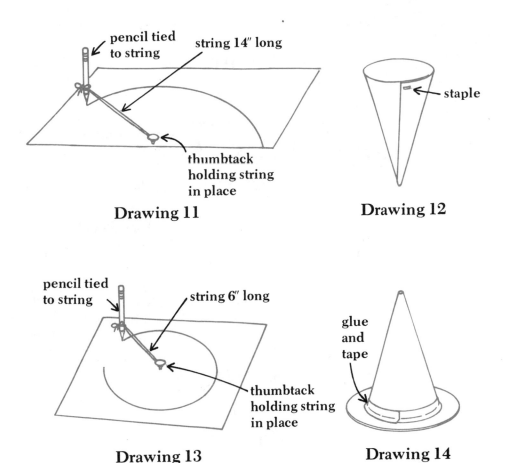

pencil tied to string

string 14″ long

thumbtack holding string in place

Drawing 11

staple

Drawing 12

pencil tied to string

string 6″ long

thumbtack holding string in place

Drawing 13

glue and tape

Drawing 14

Cut 60 to 70 pieces of yarn 12 inches long and glue them near the top of the head for hair. Drawing 10.

On black cardboard measuring at least 14 inches by 28 inches, draw a half circle 28 inches across. Drawing 11. Cut out and roll the cardboard into a cone whose base is the same size as the top of the head. (Page 183 shows how.) Staple the cone together along the bottom edge. Drawing 12.

On another piece of black cardboard draw a circle about 12 inches in diameter and cut it out. Drawing 13. Glue and tape this circle to the cone to form the hat's brim. (Color the tape black.) Drawing 14. Now glue the hat to the top of the mask.

The next page shows how you can make some other kinds of costumes—or you can think up some of your own.

KNIGHT

body front

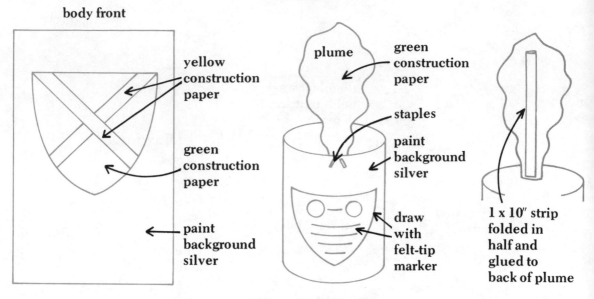

yellow construction paper

green construction paper

paint background silver

plume

green construction paper

staples

paint background silver

draw with felt-tip marker

1 x 10″ strip folded in half and glued to back of plume

Drawing 15

UNCLE SAM

body front

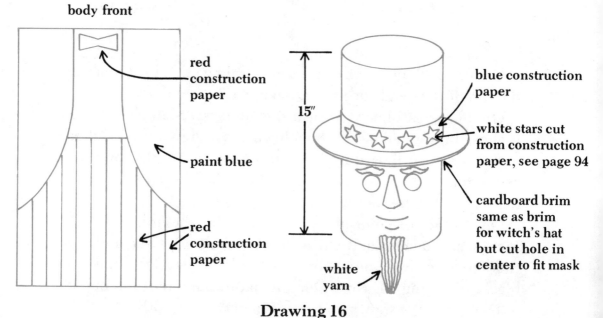

red construction paper

paint blue

red construction paper

15″

blue construction paper

white stars cut from construction paper, see page 94

cardboard brim same as brim for witch's hat but cut hole in center to fit mask

white yarn

Drawing 16

108

Picture Puzzle

Materials: newspapers to cover work space; picture from old magazine; construction paper; typing paper; paste. Tools: books; scissors.

PICTURE PUZZLES are fun to put together. To make one:

Cut out a picture from an old magazine. Then cut out a piece of construction paper slightly larger than the picture. Now cut out a sheet of typing paper the same size as the construction paper. Paste the typing paper to one side of the construction paper and the picture to the other. Smooth out both sides with your hands and place the pasted-up picture under heavy books.

Allow 30 minutes for the paste to dry and then trim the construction paper so it is the same size as the picture. Now cut the mounted picture into about 12 pieces. You can cut them as shown above or you can make each a different shape.

Mix up the pieces and put your picture puzzle back together.

Indian Drum

Materials: two-pound coffee can with plastic lid; masking tape; two sheets of construction paper; transparent tape; two wire coat hangers with cardboard tubes. Tools: ruler; pencil; scissors; crayons. Optional: tracing paper; carbon paper.

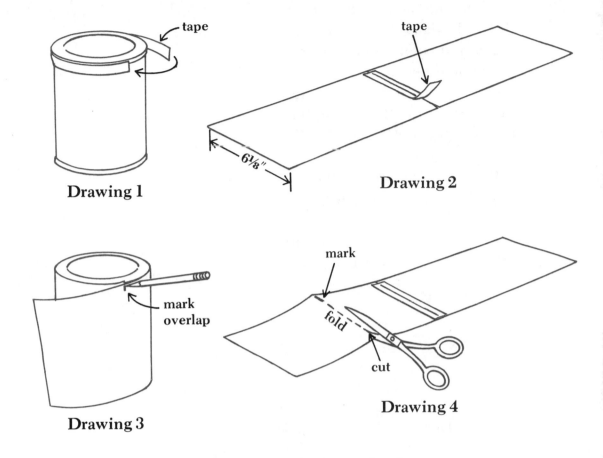

Drawing 1

Drawing 2

Drawing 3

Drawing 4

ALMOST ALL INDIAN TRIBES used drums for dancing, singing, and signaling. One of their favorite kinds was the water drum—a drum partly filled with water to make it sound better. To send an Indian message on your own water drum:

Pour ³/₄ inch of water into an empty two-pound coffee can. (Stand a ruler in the can to measure the water as you pour.)

Put the can's plastic lid on tight and tape it all the way around with masking tape. See Drawing 1.

Cut two long strips, each 6¹/₈ inches wide, out of two sheets of construction paper. Tape the two strips together lengthwise. Drawing 2.

Place this long strip around the can and mark the strip where one end overlaps the other. Drawing 3.

Remove the paper and fold it at the place you marked. Cut along the fold to remove the overlapping end. Drawing 4.

With the taped side down, draw Indian designs on the paper and color them with crayons. Some designs you can use are shown in Drawing 5. Draw them, or trace them and then transfer them. (Pages 184 and 185 show how.)

Put the paper around the can. Tape the seam with transparent tape.

For drumsticks, use cardboard tubes from wire coat hangers.

mountains

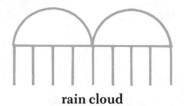
rain cloud

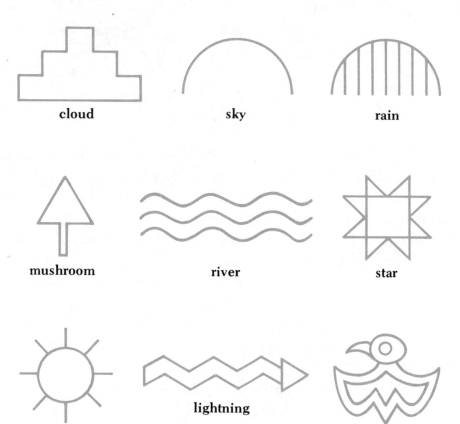

cloud   sky   rain

mushroom   river   star

sun   lightning   bird

Drawing 5

Peep Show

Materials: newspapers to cover work space; shoe box with cover; old magazine; white glue; plastic figures, such as farm animals, cowboys, or soldiers. Tools: ruler; pencil; scissors; thumbtack. Optional: paint and brush; colored cellophane, such as the kind used to wrap hard candy; masking tape.

BEFORE THERE WERE MOVIES, there were peep shows.

Only one person at a time could see the show, by peeping into a kind of box that held the pictures. Surprise your audience with a scene from a peep show!

In or near the center of a shoe box cover, draw a rectangle 2 inches long and 1 inch wide. (Page 180 shows how.) Have an older person help you cut out the rectangle. See Drawing 1.

To make a peephole, push a thumbtack through one end of the box and enlarge it with a pencil. The hole should be about the same size as the pencil. Drawing 2.

In a magazine find a colored picture to use for the background inside the box. Look for one that goes well with the kind of figures you will use in your peep show. For instance, if the figures are farm animals, find a picture of a farm or field.

Stand the box on its end on the picture. Draw a line on the picture around the box. Drawing 3. Cut out the picture and glue it inside the box at the end opposite the peephole. Drawing 4.

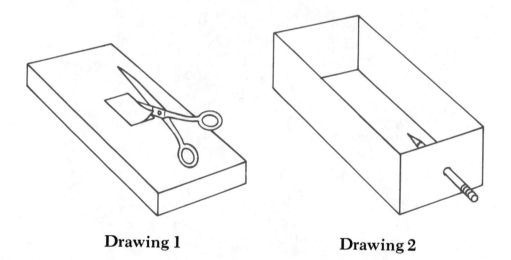

Drawing 1   Drawing 2

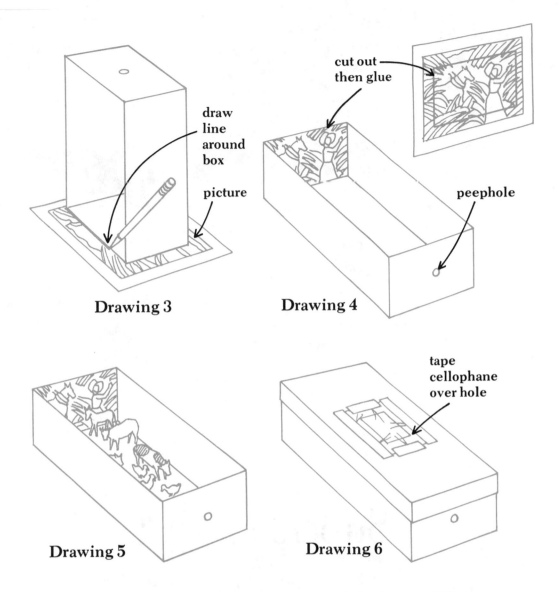

Drawing 3

draw line around box

picture

Drawing 4

cut out then glue

peephole

Drawing 5

Drawing 6

tape cellophane over hole

Glue the plastic figures to the bottom of the box at different distances from the picture. Drawing 5. Put the cover on the box.

If you wish, paint the outside of the box.

When you look through the peephole at the show, hold the box up to the light. You might have to move the box around a little to get the light just right. You can also use the box outdoors in the sun, or shine a flashlight through the top hole.

If you want to change the color of your peep show scene, cut colored cellophane larger than the top hole. Tape it over the hole with masking tape. Drawing 6.

Supersonic Jet

Materials: newspapers to cover work space; long cardboard tube (from a roll of gift-wrapping paper or wide aluminum foil); lightweight cardboard; masking tape; white glue; paint (two or three colors); modeling clay. Tools: ruler; scissors; pencil; compass or other circle maker; paintbrush.

SUPERSONIC JETS fly faster than sound. This model won't fly that fast, but it will cruise far and high if you take time to put it together carefully. Follow the directions for each step exactly.

For the jet's body, use a cardboard tube 15 inches long or cut a longer tube to this size. Then cut a 13-inch-long slot in the tube, starting at one end. See Drawing 1.

For the nose of the jet, draw a half circle that is 9 inches across, on lightweight cardboard. If you do not have a compass, you can use half of a 9-inch paper plate as a guide. Drawing 2.

Cut out the half circle and roll it into a cone. (Page 183 shows how.) The bottom of the cone should measure about $2^1/4$ inches across. Tape the seam. Cut pointed notches about 1 inch deep all around the bottom of the cone. Drawing 3.

Fit the cone on the unslotted end of the tube, with the ends of the notches coming to within 1 inch of the slot. Glue and tape the cone in place. The tape should begin about $1/4$ inch from the slot and form a band about 2 inches wide. Drawing 4.

Paint the tube and cone, but not the tape.

For wings, cut a piece of cardboard to measure $8^1/2$ inches by

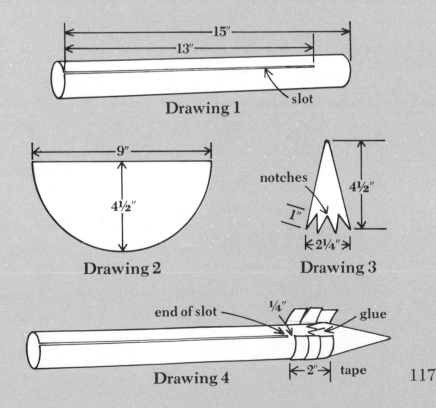

Drawing 1

Drawing 2

Drawing 3

Drawing 4

117

11 inches. (Page 180 shows how.) Draw lines A, B, and C as shown in Drawing 5.

Fold a piece toward you along line A and away from you along line B. These folds will form tabs. Now cut the piece apart along line C. Drawing 6.

Put the two tabs (folded parts) together to form a big triangle and glue them together. Drawing 7. Then put glue on the outer sides of this tab. Drawing 8. Slide the wing piece through the slot up to the nose of the plane. Tape around the plane's body behind the wing piece, forming a band about 1½ inches wide. Drawing 9.

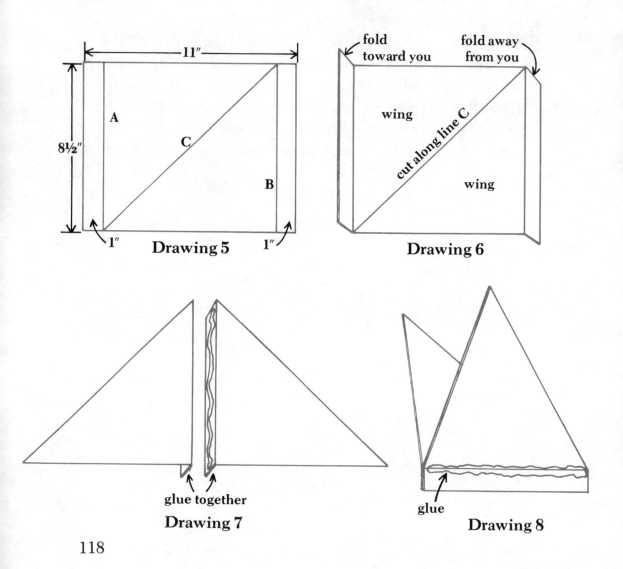

118

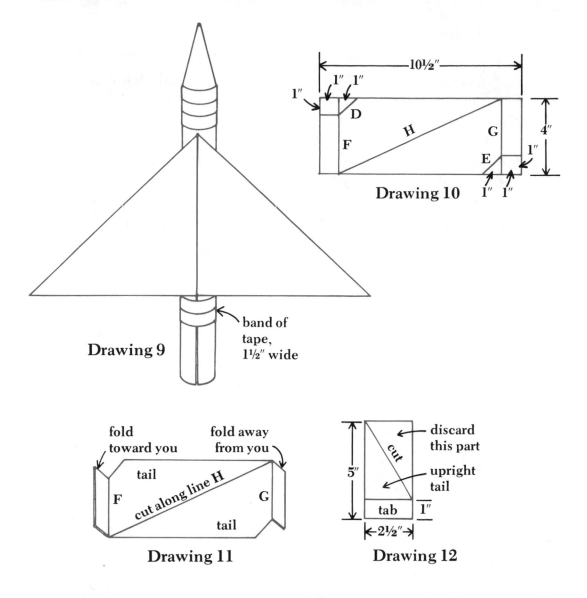

Drawing 9

band of
tape,
1½″ wide

Drawing 10

Drawing 11

fold
toward you

fold away
from you

tail

cut along line H

F

tail

G

Drawing 12

discard
this part

cut

upright
tail

5″

tab   1″

2½″

For the tail, cut out a piece of cardboard measuring 4 inches by 10½ inches. Draw lines D, E, F, G, and H as shown in Drawing 10.

Cut along lines D and E. Fold toward you along line F and away from you along line G to form tabs. Now cut the pieces apart along line H. Drawing 11. These two pieces are tail pieces. Do not glue yet.

For an upright tail piece, cut out a piece of cardboard measuring 2½ inches by 5 inches. Draw lines as shown in Drawing 12 and cut along the diagonal line. Discard the part without the tab.

119

Put glue on both sides of the 1-inch tab. Sandwich this tab between the tabs of the other two tail pieces as shown in Drawing 13.

Put glue on both sides of this glued-together tab. Slide the tab into the body slot until it meets the tape. Drawing 14.

Paint the wings and tail one color and the tape another color.

Test your jet in a grassy area away from trees. Test fly it several times and observe the way it behaves. If it tends to stall, add some modeling clay to the nose. If it tends to dive, add clay to the tail. Drawing 15.

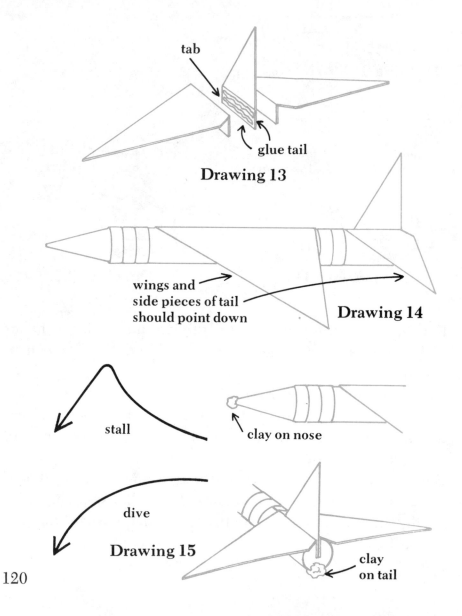

tab

glue tail

Drawing 13

wings and
side pieces of tail
should point down

Drawing 14

stall

clay on nose

dive

Drawing 15

clay
on tail

Paper Plate
Monster

Materials: newspapers to cover work space; two paper plates; white glue; egg carton; six pipe cleaners; red construction paper; paint. Tools: scissors; paintbrush.

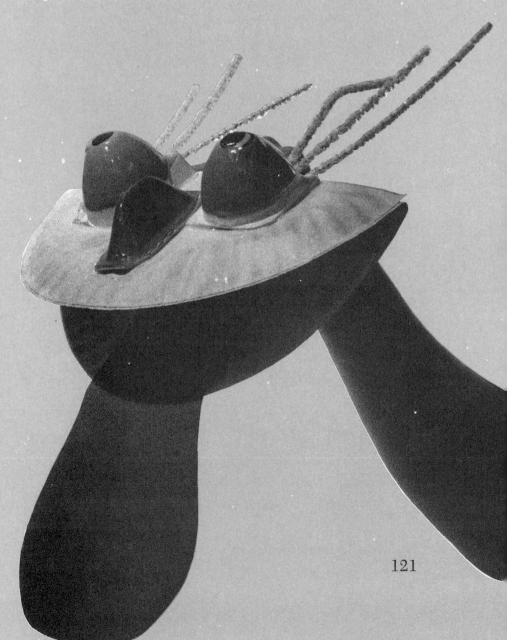

THIS MONSTER is a hand puppet. You can make it talk, chew, laugh, and growl. To create a monster of your very own:

Fold a paper plate in half, with the eating surface on the inside. See Drawing 1.

To make a face, cut a second paper plate in half. Discard one half. Drawing 2. With the other half right-side-up, put glue on the rim. Drawing 3. Press the glued side onto the outside of one

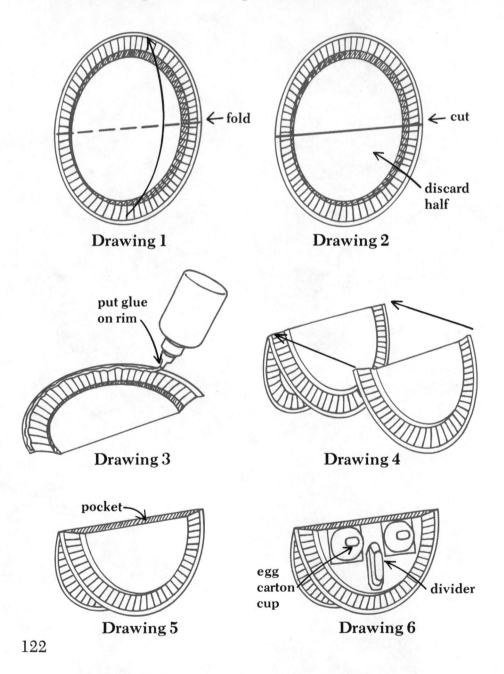

Drawing 1 ← fold

Drawing 2 ← cut
discard half

Drawing 3 put glue on rim

Drawing 4

Drawing 5 pocket

Drawing 6 egg carton cup — divider

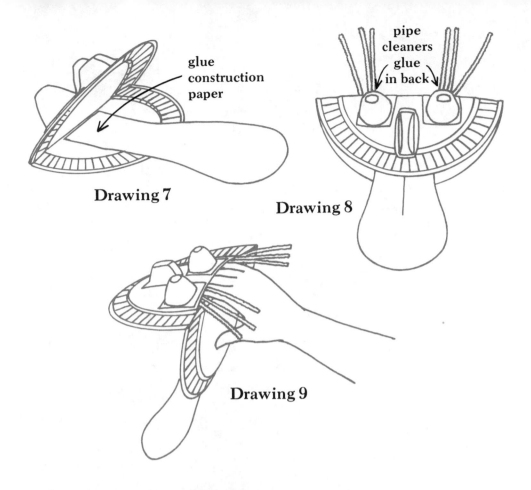

glue
construction
paper

Drawing 7

pipe
cleaners
glue
in back

Drawing 8

Drawing 9

of the folded halves, rims touching. Drawing 4. This forms a thin pocket. Drawing 5.

Cut two egg cups from an egg carton and glue them onto the face for eyes. Cut a cup divider from the egg carton and glue it on for the nose. Drawing 6.

Cut a large tongue from red construction paper. Glue the base of it inside of the folded plate, on the lower half, so that it hangs out. Drawing 7.

Glue three pipe cleaners upright above each eye, on the back of the face inside the pocket. Drawing 8.

Paint the plate, nose, and eyes different colors. When the eyes are dry, add a dab of black paint to the center of each for pupils.

You can work your monster's mouth by putting your fingers in the thin pocket and using your thumb on the back of the lower half. Drawing 9. To move the mouth, press your fingers and thumb together and then move them apart.

Tie-Dye Design

Materials: old T-shirt; string; package of dye. Tools: large old pan; clean stick for stirring; iron.

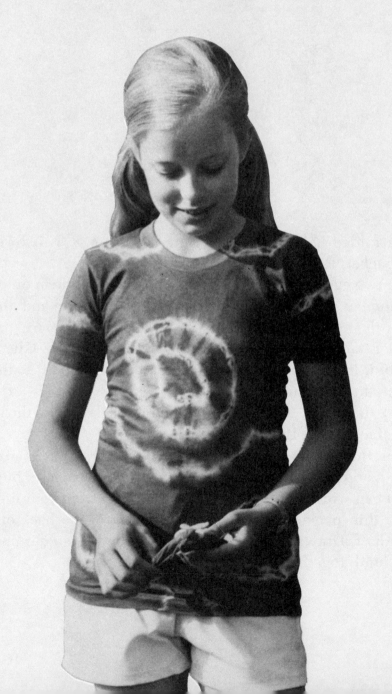

TIE-DYEING IS DONE by people of all countries. It is a very old way of making designs on cloth. It probably started in India, where some of the finest tie-dyeing is done. The cloth under a tightly tied string won't take dye. The part that is not dyed makes the design. The design you get this way will surprise you.

Spread an old T-shirt out flat. Gather it in the center, gathering front and back in the same handful. Wrap string around the gathered piece several times. Tie the string with a bow so that you can untie it easily later. See Drawing 1.

Continue gathering and tying, as many times as you can. Drawing 2 shows how to get a balanced design—you match each tie on the left side with one on the right side.

Mix dye in an old pan, following the directions that come with the package. Use very hot water.

Put the whole T-shirt under water. Stir with a clean stick until the T-shirt is as dark as you want it. Rinse in cold water and wring out. Untie the strings and hang the shirt up to dry.

Have the shirt ironed to make the dye more permanent. Whenever you wash the shirt, use cool water.

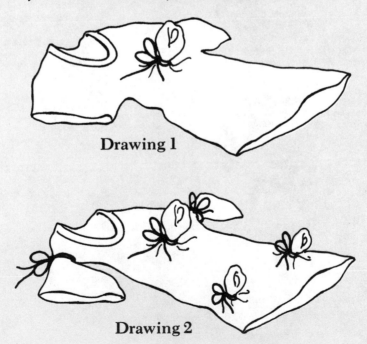

Drawing 1

Drawing 2

Pipe
Cleaner
Monkey

Materials: pipe cleaners; straws or sticks; heavy string. Tools: scissors. Optional: transparent tape or masking tape; moderately heavy wire.

HERE IS A PET that never needs to be fed:

Bend one pipe cleaner as shown in Drawing 1. Then bend a second pipe cleaner as shown in Drawing 2.

Wind the second pipe cleaner twice around the first one, near the top. Drawing 3.

Bend a third pipe cleaner as shown in Drawing 4. Wind it twice around the first one, farther down. Drawing 5.

Wind another pipe cleaner around the monkey's middle. Drawing 6.

Monkeys are expert climbers and love to swing. To make a swing for your monkey:

Cut a straw in half (or use two small sticks). Cut off two pieces of heavy string, each about as long as a straw.

Tie the string near the ends of the straws. Wrap your monkey's hand around one straw.

To hang your monkey's swing, stick a piece of transparent tape or masking tape to the top straw. You can tape the swing to the edge of a table or shelf, the back of a chair, a door, or a window frame. Or make a hook out of wire and hang the swing from a light fixture.

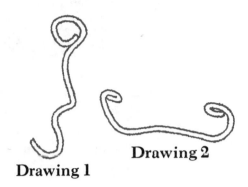

Drawing 2

Drawing 1

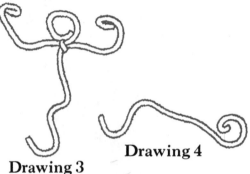

Drawing 3

Drawing 4

Drawing 5

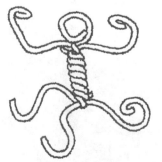

Drawing 6   127

Jumping Jack

Materials: newspapers to cover work space; tracing paper; masking tape; medium-weight cardboard; six paper fasteners (#1 size); flat stick about 6 inches long; white glue; heavy thread. Tools: pencil; felt-tip markers or crayons; scissors; paper punch; thumbtack. Optional: carbon paper.

JACK WAS ALREADY A FAVORITE with children when your grandparents were young. You'll know why when you pull the string and see the way Jack jumps for you. Here is how to put him together:

Trace the pattern from Drawing 1. Be sure to include the 12 circles and 4 dots. Transfer the tracing onto cardboard. (Pages 184 and 185 show how.)

Color the jumping jack and cut out the cardboard. With a paper punch, punch out the 12 circles.

128

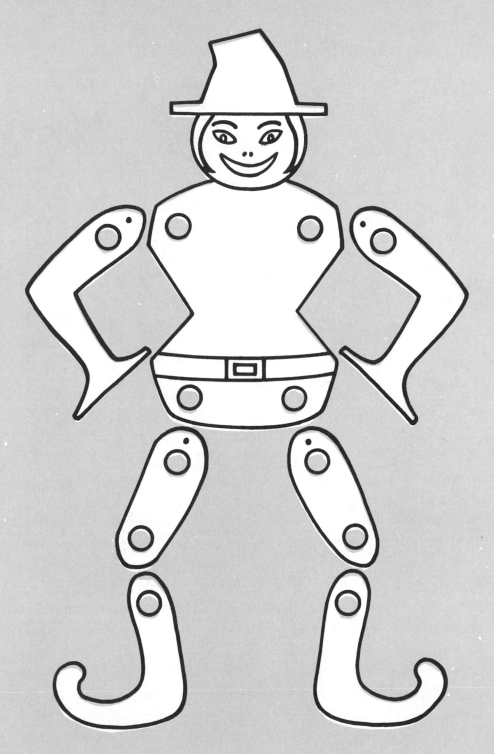

Drawing 1

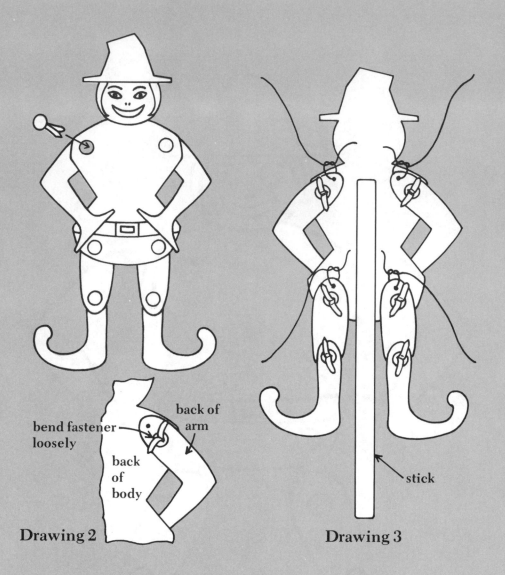

bend fastener loosely

back of arm

back of body

Drawing 2

stick

Drawing 3

With a thumbtack, punch holes on the dots in the arms and legs.

Attach the arms and legs to the body with paper fasteners. The fasteners should be bent back loosely, so that the arms and legs move freely. Drawing 2.

Glue the back of the body to a stick as shown in Drawing 3.

Cut four 4-inch-long pieces of heavy thread. Thread one piece through the small hole in one of the arms, and tie. (If the hole is too small, make it bigger with a pencil point.) Repeat with the other arm and with the small holes in both legs. Drawing 3.

130

Tie the two arm threads together at Jack's back as shown in Drawing 4. Cut off the loose ends below the knot. Do the same with the two leg threads.

Cut a piece of thread about 6 inches long. Use it to join the arm and leg threads at the back as shown in Drawing 5. Let the end of this thread hang down.

To make Jack jump, hold the stick in one hand and pull the hanging thread with the other hand.

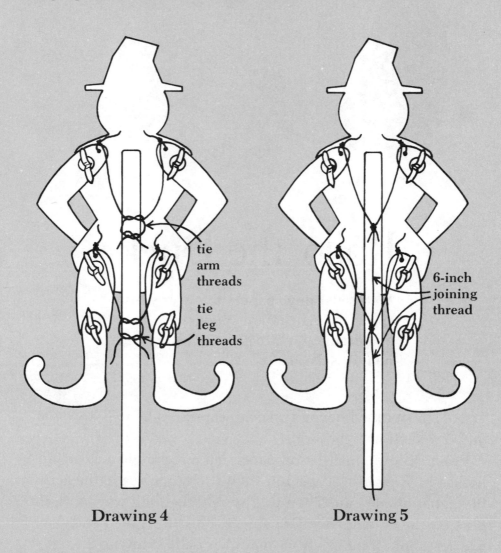

tie arm threads

tie leg threads

6-inch joining thread

Drawing 4　　　　　　**Drawing 5**

Rollo the Duck

Materials: newspapers to cover work space; construction paper (yellow and orange); white glue. Tools: ruler; pencil; scissors.

HERE'S A DUCK who won't go near water. But he will look good on your shelf or windowsill.

From yellow construction paper, cut a rectangle measuring 4 inches by 8 inches. (Page 180 shows how.) Spread glue across the paper at one end. Then roll loosely the long way, with the glue on the outside. See Drawing 1. Press the glued end down to stick about 2 inches from the other end. Drawing 2.

Make zigzag cuts in the loose end to look like a duck's tail feathers. Drawing 3.

Cut another piece of yellow paper, 2 inches by 4 inches. Roll it loosely the long way and glue one end on top of the other. Drawing 4.

Glue the small roll on top of the large one as shown in the photograph.

Using orange construction paper, cut out two eyes in a diamond shape. Also cut out an orange beak and two orange feet. Drawing 5 shows how to shape and fold them.

Glue these parts onto the duck as shown in the photograph.

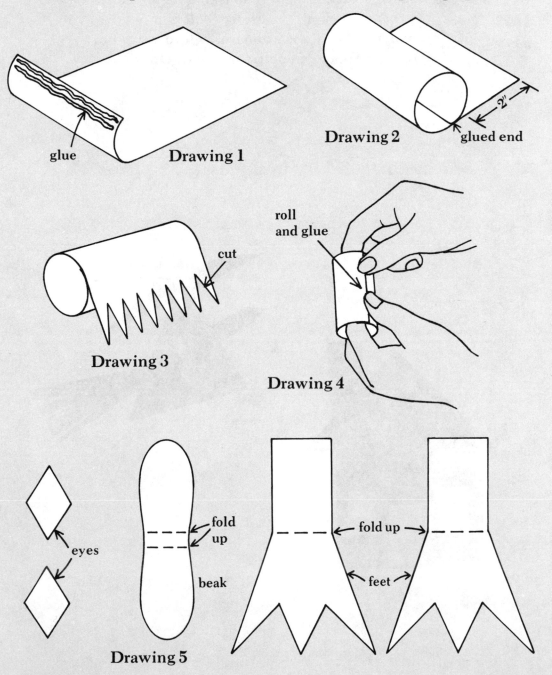

glue   **Drawing 1**

Drawing 2   glued end   2"

roll and glue

cut

Drawing 3

Drawing 4

eyes

fold up

beak

fold up

feet

Drawing 5

Cut and Paste

Materials: newspapers to cover work space; tracing paper; masking tape; construction paper (various colors); white paper or white cardboard; white glue or paste. Tools: pencil; scissors. Optional: carbon paper.

Cᴜᴛ, ᴘᴀꜱᴛᴇ, and you have a picture!

Trace the shapes for the witch or for one of the pictures on the next two pages. Transfer the tracings to construction paper. (Pages 184 and 185 show how.) Cut the shapes out. Move them into place on a piece of white paper or cardboard.

When the cutouts form a picture you like, glue or paste them in place.

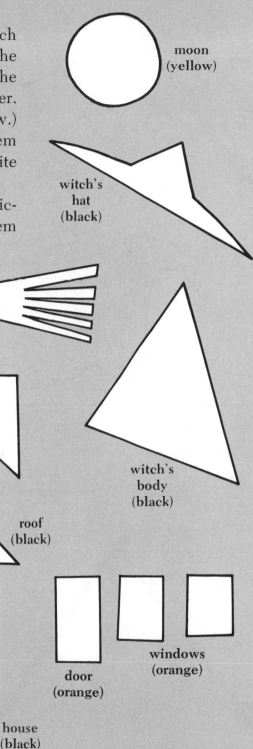

WITCH

moon
(yellow)

witch's
hat
(black)

broom
(black)

chimney
(black)

witch's
body
(black)

roof
(black)

door
(orange)

windows
(orange)

house
(black)

FISHERMAN

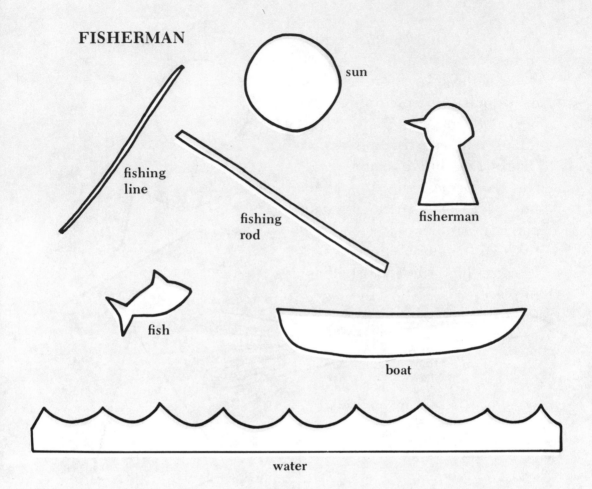

sun

fishing
line

fishing
rod

fisherman

fish

boat

water

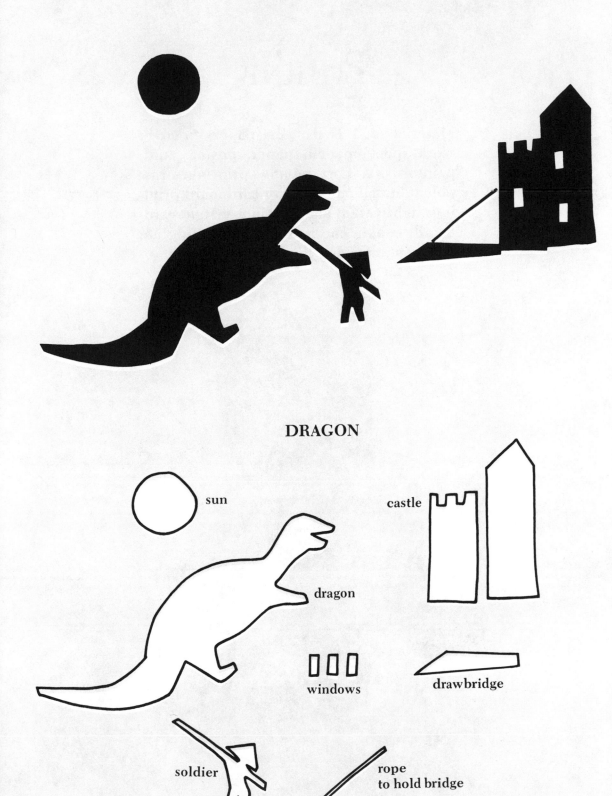

DRAGON

sun

dragon

castle

windows

drawbridge

soldier

rope
to hold bridge

137

Printing

Materials and Tools: newspapers to cover work space; pencil; paper; poster paint; paintbrush. For potato printing: raw potato; metal nail file. For cardboard printing: lightweight and medium-weight cardboard; cookie cutter; scissors; white glue; books; shellac and thinner; rolling pin.

ONE WAY OF PRINTING is to use a raised design or letter. You put paint on the raised part and then press it on paper. This is the oldest way of printing and is still common today.

Potato printing is one way to print with a raised design. Here is how you do it:

Have an older person cut a potato in half. With a pencil draw a design on the flat, cut side of one half. See Drawing 1.

Then, with the handle of a nail file, cut away all the parts of the flat side that are not in your design. Cut about 1/4 inch deep. This will leave your design raised about 1/4 inch. Drawing 2.

Cover the raised design with poster paint. Drawing 3. Then press the potato, design side down, on paper. Drawing 4.

Try repeating your design in a pattern. In making the pattern you can use several different colors. Or you can add a second or third design, each in a different color.

Be sure to clean your paintbrush in water when you are done.

Drawing 1

Drawing 2

metal nail file

Drawing 3

Drawing 4

Another way to make a raised design is to build it up in layers. Use a cookie cutter or other object as a pattern. Put it on lightweight cardboard and draw around it. Make five separate drawings. Drawing 5.

Cut out the five drawings and glue them one on top of the other. Drawing 6. Put the stack under heavy books and let it dry there for about 15 minutes.

Glue the stack to a square of medium-weight cardboard. Make the square large enough for you to hold in your hand easily. Brush shellac on the top and edges of the stack. Drawing 7. Clean your brush in thinner.

When the top and edges of the stack are dry, brush poster paint on the top. Drawing 8. Place the painted side down on paper. Move a rolling pin over the back of the square, pressing down slightly. Drawing 9. Lift the printing block carefully to

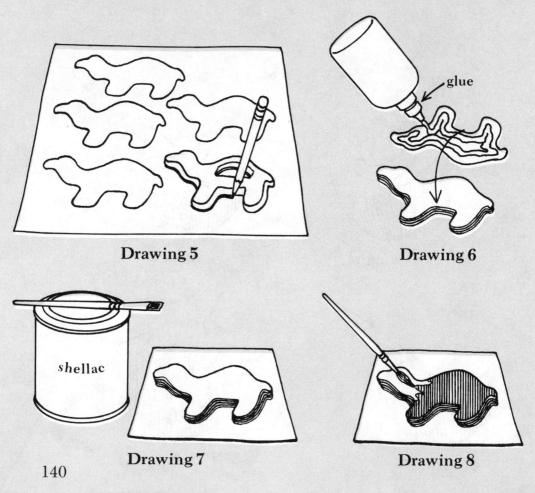

Drawing 5

Drawing 6

glue

Drawing 7

shellac

Drawing 8

140

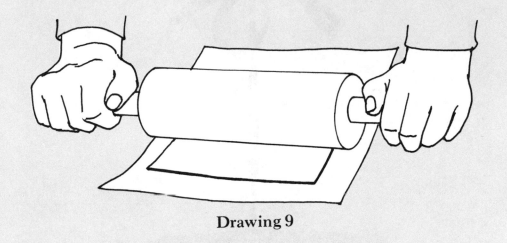

Drawing 9

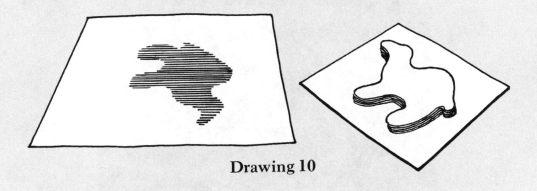

Drawing 10

avoid smearing. If the printed image is spotty, you didn't press hard enough on the rolling pin. If its outline is smeared, you pressed too hard.

Notice how the printed camel in Drawing 10 is facing the opposite direction from the camel on the printing block. All printing block designs are backwards. Do you know why?

You can use this kind of printing to make your own pictures and posters. You can also make your own gift-wrapping paper, note paper, and greeting cards.

For gift-wrapping paper, print designs on big sheets of colored or white paper.

For note paper, fold a sheet of typing paper in half. Print a design across the top or down one side.

For a greeting card, cut a piece of construction paper so it will fit inside an envelope. Print a design on the left side and write your message next to it.

141

Paper
Picture Plaque

Materials: newspapers to cover
work space; paper plates; old magazines; white glue; yarn; adhesive
tape. **Tools:** scissors; pencil; crayons.

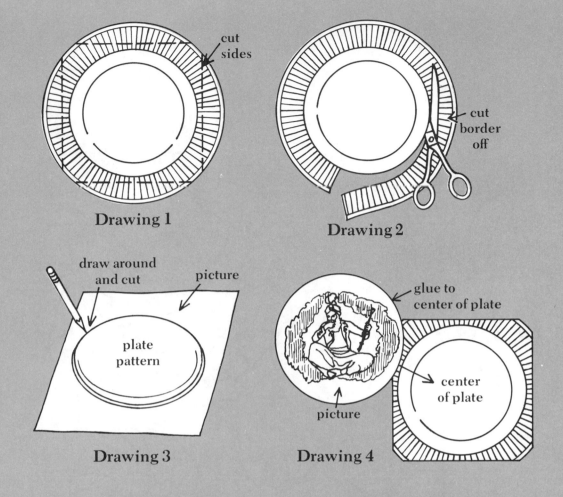

Drawing 1

Drawing 2

Drawing 3

Drawing 4

A PLAQUE is a wall decoration. Here's one made with a picture and paper plate.

Cut the sides of a paper plate as shown in the photograph and in Drawing 1.

Cut the border off a second paper plate, leaving only the flat round center. Drawing 2. Use this center as a pattern to draw a circle over the picture you want to use. Drawing 3. Cut out the picture along this circle and glue to the center of the square plate. Drawing 4.

Color the border on the plate with crayons as shown in the photograph.

For a hanger use a double piece of yarn. Tie a bow at one end. Attach the other end to the back of the plaque with adhesive tape.

Christmas Patterns

Pages 184 and 185 show how to trace and transfer patterns.

144

145

Paper
Snowflakes

Materials: typing paper or construction paper. Tools: pencil; ruler; scissors.

146

SNOWFLAKE 1

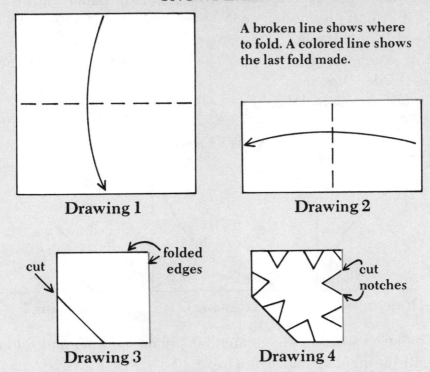

A broken line shows where to fold. A colored line shows the last fold made.

Drawing 1

Drawing 2

cut

folded edges

Drawing 3

cut notches

Drawing 4

EACH SNOWFLAKE THAT FALLS from the sky is different from all other snowflakes. Each has a slightly different size and pattern, though they all have six sides.

Four different kinds of snowflakes are shown here for you to make. The first three do not have six sides like real snowflakes, but are easier to make than the six-sided kind.

You can use your snowflakes, in white or colors, to trim your Christmas tree and brighten your holiday cards and packages. Glue or tape them on cards and packages, and hang them from the tree by first attaching a loop of thread.

To make snowflake 1, cut a square of paper (page 181 shows how) and fold the square in half. See Drawing 1. Then fold it in half again. Drawing 2.

Hold the paper so that the folded edges are at top and right. Cut off the lower left corner. Drawing 3.

Then cut notches all around. Drawing 4. Leave at least one small part uncut on each folded side. Open your snowflake.

147

To make snowflake 2, cut another square of paper. This time fold it in half on the diagonal. Drawing 5.

Fold it in half again. Drawing 6.

Cut notches, leaving at least one small part uncut on each folded side. Drawing 7.

Open your snowflake.

SNOWFLAKE 2

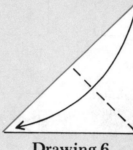
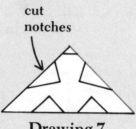

Drawing 5   **Drawing 6**   **Drawing 7**

To make snowflake 3, cut another square of paper and fold it in half on the diagonal. Drawing 8.

Fold it in half again. Drawing 9.

Cut a quarter circle around the unfolded edge. Then fold the paper in half again. Drawing 10.

Cut notches, leaving at least one small part uncut on each folded side. Drawing 11.

Open your snowflake.

SNOWFLAKE 3

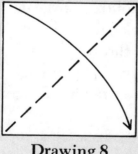
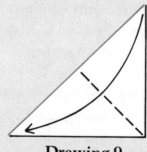

Drawing 8   **Drawing 9**

148

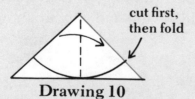

Drawing 10   **Drawing 11**

To make a six-sided snowflake, cut out a square measuring about 8 inches on each side. Fold in half. Drawing 12.

Fold in half again, to form a square. Drawing 13.

Fold the square in half. Drawing 14. Then unfold, so that you have a rectangle again. Drawing 15.

As shown in Drawing 16, fold corner A up to make a diagonal fold running from the top of crease B to the bottom of crease C.

Now fold the other part up so that side D rests along side E. Drawing 17.

Your paper should now look like Drawing 18.

Turn the paper over and fold in half as shown in Drawing 19.

Make a wavy cut below the line marked with the colored arrow in Drawing 20. Then cut out notches, but be sure that several portions along the two long sides are not cut out.

Unfold the paper and you have a six-sided snowflake.

SIX-SIDED SNOWFLAKE

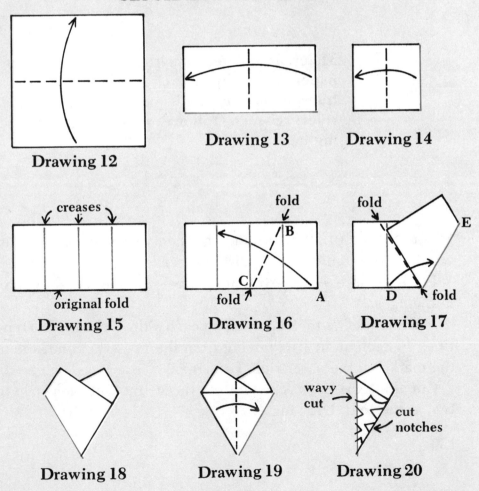

Drawing 12

Drawing 13

Drawing 14

Drawing 15

Drawing 16

Drawing 17

Drawing 18

Drawing 19

Drawing 20

Paper Chains

Materials: colored construction paper (9 inch by 12 inch size); transparent tape. Tools: pencil; ruler; scissors. Optional: masking tape.

MAKE COLORFUL CHAINS and hang them on a wall, across your window, or around your Christmas tree.

Fold a piece of construction paper in half as shown in Drawing 1.

Make marks ³/₄ inch apart along each side. Drawing 2. Draw lines ³/₄ inch apart by drawing from the marks on one side to the marks on the other side. Drawing 3.

Cut along the lines. Then unfold the strips. Cut each strip in two at the fold. Drawing 4.

Take one strip and tape the ends together. Drawing 5. Then take another strip and slip it through the loop of the first strip. Drawing 6. Tape its ends together. Keep on adding loops until your chain is as long as you wish.

You can make your chain all one color or you can make the loops different colors. If you hang your chain from a wall, use small pieces of masking tape. Transparent tape might peel off the paint or wallpaper when you remove it.

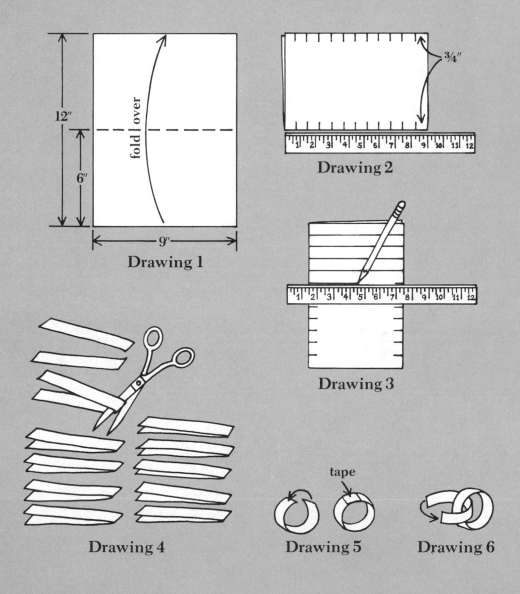

Drawing 1

Drawing 2

Drawing 3

Drawing 4

tape

Drawing 5

Drawing 6

Homemade Clay

Materials for clay: baking soda; cornstarch; water. Tools: cooking pan (1 quart) with tight-fitting lid; measuring cup; tablespoon or other stirrer. Materials for ornaments and pendants: homemade clay; paper clips or toothpick (or both); newspapers; plastic model paint (or enamel paint) and thinner; yarn. Tools: rolling pin; cookie cutters; spatula; cake rack; small paintbrush; scissors. Optional: pictures from old magazines; white glue.

THIS SPECIAL CLAY is like the kind sculptors use. It gets hard when it dries. Use it for making ornaments, statues, jewelry, and other things you want to keep or give as gifts. It is best to work with this clay only on a dry day. If the air is damp, the clay is likely to crumble. To make clay:

Use a cooking pan that has a lid. Pour exactly 2 cups of baking soda and 1 cup of cornstarch into the pan. Add exactly 1¼ cups of water.

Put the pan on the stove over medium heat and stir. The mixture will be hard to stir at first. Keep stirring until it feels and looks about like mashed potatoes. This will take about 5 minutes.

Take the pan off the stove. Cover it with a tight-fitting lid, and put it in the refrigerator for 45 minutes. Your clay will then be lukewarm and ready to use.

To use the clay to make Christmas tree ornaments, you will need cookie cutters of several different shapes, such as the shapes shown in the photographs on the opposite page.

Knead the clay with your hands to make it easy to work. Place the clay on a bread board or counter top. With a rolling pin, roll it out to about the thickness of a pencil. Drawing 1.

With a cookie cutter, cut one "clay cookie" for each ornament you want to make. Drawing 2.

To make a simple hanger, use a toothpick to make a hole in each ornament near its edge. Make the hole large enough for

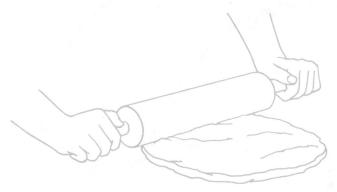

Drawing 1

Drawing 2

yarn to pass through, so you can hang the ornament on your tree. Then use a spatula to place the ornaments on a cake rack to dry.

You can also make a fancier hanger. Don't make a hole, but, instead, pick up the ornament with a spatula and put it flat in the palm of your hand. Then carefully push one end of a paper clip, flat side up, inside the ornament at its top. Then place the ornament on a cake rack.

Let the ornament dry for 24 hours.

Cover your work space with newspapers and paint each ornament's front and sides. Let the paint dry. Then, if you're good at drawing, paint on your own design. Or you can paint on polka dots of another color, or glue on colorful pictures cut out of a magazine. Be sure to clean your brushes.

For a hanger, cut a piece of yarn about 12 inches long. Thread it through the hole or paper clip and tie the ends.

You can also use clay to make a pendant. A pendant is a special kind of ornament—one that hangs around your neck. Make a whole batch and give them as presents. Use a round cookie cutter and follow the same directions as for clay ornaments. Make the yarn hanger long enough to fit around your neck.

Clay Angel

Materials: homemade clay (see page 152); lightweight cardboard; tape; red birthday cake candle; newspapers; plastic model paint (or enamel paint) and thinner; yellow construction paper; white glue. Tools: ruler; compass or other circle maker; rolling pin; paintbrush; pencil; scissors.

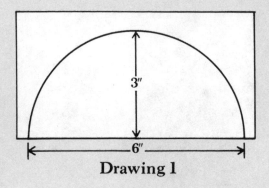

Drawing 1

HERE IS AN ANGEL to bring Christmas to your table. But start early; it has to rest for two or three days before you paint it.

Draw a half circle with a diameter of about 6 inches on a piece of cardboard. Drawing 1. Cut out the half circle and roll it into a cone. (Page 183 shows how.) Tape the cone together. Drawing 2.

Knead the clay with your hands. With a rolling pin roll out a piece of clay about $\frac{1}{16}$ inch thick and large enough to cover the cone. Smooth it onto the cone after wetting your fingers. Drawing 3. Patch holes by adding more clay with wet fingers.

For the angel's hands, roll two pieces of clay into two

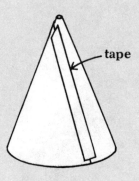

tape

Drawing 2

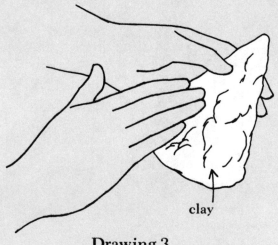

clay

Drawing 3

Drawing 4

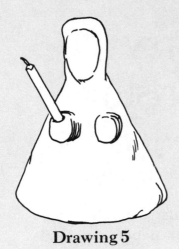

Drawing 5

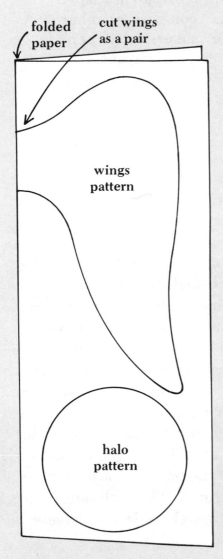

folded paper

cut wings as a pair

wings pattern

halo pattern

Drawing 6

balls about ¹/₂ inch in diameter. Stick them to the front of the cone. Stick a red candle into one hand. Drawing 4.

For the head, make a larger ball—about 1 inch in diameter—and smooth it into the top of the cone. Mold it with wet fingers. Drawing 5.

Let the angel dry for at least two days. Then cover your work space with newspapers and paint the angel. Clean your brushes.

When the paint is dry, cut wings and a halo from yellow construction paper and glue on. Drawings 6 and 7.

glue

Drawing 7

Starry Christmas Tree

Materials: green construction paper; gummed stars; transparent tape. Tools: compass or other circle maker; ruler; pencil; scissors; crayons.

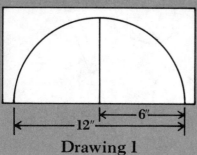

Drawing 1

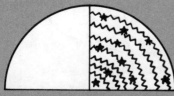

Drawing 2

HERE'S A CHRISTMAS TREE that won't shed its needles.

Draw a half circle on green construction paper. It should have a diameter of about 12 inches. Draw a line dividing the half circle into two parts. See Drawing 1.

Cut out the half circle. Color one of the two quarter circles with crayons and paste stars on. Drawing 2. Then roll into a cone and tape. (Page 183 shows how.)

Candy Cone Ornament

Materials: red construction paper; transparent tape; ribbon; hard candy. Tools: compass or other circle maker; ruler; pencil; scissors.

SOME CONES can hold ice cream—and some can hold candy. To make this candy-filled Christmas tree ornament, draw a half circle on red construction paper. Make it about 11 inches in diameter. Drawing 1. Cut out and roll into a cone and tape. (Page 183 shows how.)

Cut a piece of colored ribbon for a hanger. With a pencil tip, punch a hole in opposite sides of the cone. Pull the ribbon through the holes (Drawing 2) and tie in a bow.

You can decorate the cone with designs cut from gift-wrapping paper.

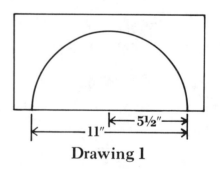

Drawing 1

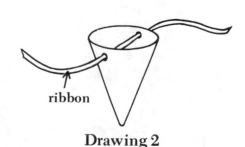

ribbon

Drawing 2

159

Easter Patterns

Pages 184 and 185 show how to trace and transfer patterns.

160

Easter Eggs

Materials: hard-boiled eggs, white or dyed; construction paper; small fruit basket. Tools: felt-tip markers.

EASTER EGGS have a meaning—they stand for new life. Decorate them bright as a spring morning. Then show them off in a colorful nest.

Page 166 tells how to make hard-boiled eggs. Draw a pattern on each egg with felt-tip markers. Draw flowers, or circles, or zigzags, or dots. Use several colors on the same egg. Let the eggs dry on a piece of paper.

To make a nest for the eggs, cut colored construction paper into narrow strips. Put the strips in a basket. Then put your eggs on top of the strips in the basket.

Yarn Chick

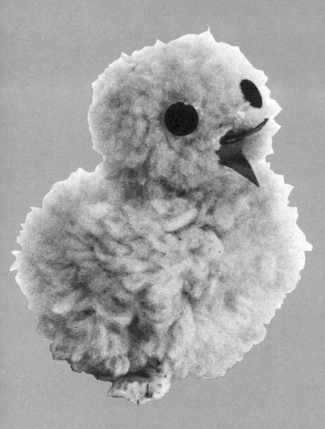

Materials: newspapers to cover work space; medium-weight cardboard; yellow yarn; white glue; red and black construction paper; pipe cleaner. **Tools:** ruler; pencil; scissors.

THIS FLUFFY CHICK can perch on your table or nest in your Easter basket. Here is how to wind him up out of yarn:

Cut two pieces of cardboard, one 1½ inches by 6 inches and the other ¾ inch by 3 inches. (Page 180 shows how.)

Cut a piece of yellow yarn about 12 inches long. Place it along the middle of the larger piece of cardboard, running the long way. This is your tying yarn.

Wind yarn around the cardboard the short way about 100 times, crossing the tying yarn each time. See Drawing 1.

Make a loose half knot in the tying yarn and slip the yarn off the cardboard. Drawing 2.

Now tighten the tying yarn and make a full knot.

Cut the yarn loops. Drawing 3. Trim the ends into a smooth, round ball. This is the chick's body.

In the same way, make a smaller ball for the chick's head.

162

Use the smaller piece of cardboard. Make the tying yarn about 6 inches long. Wind about 50 times. Drawing 4.

Glue the chick's head onto its body as shown in the photograph.

From construction paper, cut out a red beak and two little round, black eyes. They should be about the same size as Drawing 5. Glue them to the head as shown in the photograph.

Cut two 2-inch-long sections of pipe cleaner and twist each as shown in Drawing 6. Then stick the pipe cleaners in the bottom front of the body for feet. Drawing 7.

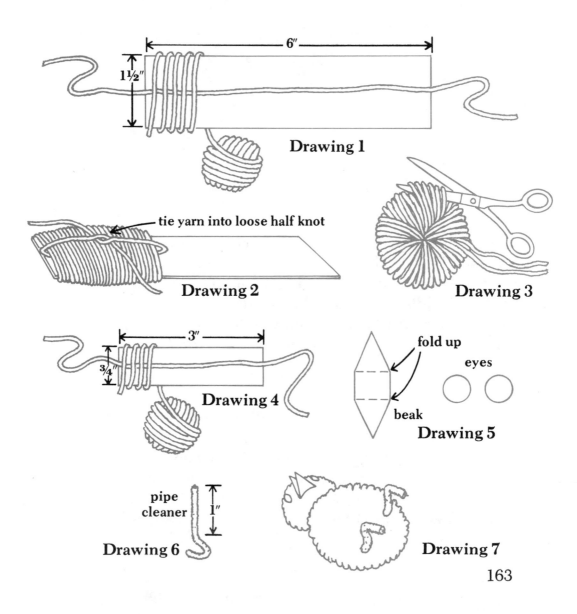

6″

1½″

Drawing 1

tie yarn into loose half knot

Drawing 2

Drawing 3

3″

¾″

Drawing 4

fold up

eyes

beak

Drawing 5

pipe cleaner

1″

Drawing 6

Drawing 7

Funny Bunny

Materials: newspapers to cover work space; pink and black construction paper; transparent tape; masking tape; tracing paper; white glue; three broom straws; cotton ball. Tools: compass or other circle maker; ruler; pencil; scissors; black felt-tip marker.

THE COMING OF THE EASTER BUNNY is a sign of spring. To make spring come early this year:

Draw a half circle on pink construction paper. Make it about 11 inches in diameter. See Drawing 1. Cut out and roll into a cone measuring about 5 inches across the open end. (Page 183 shows how.) Tape. With a black felt-tip marker, draw eyes, a nose, and feet on the cone.

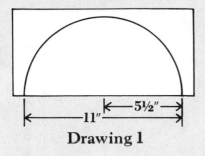

Drawing 1

11" ←———→ 5½"

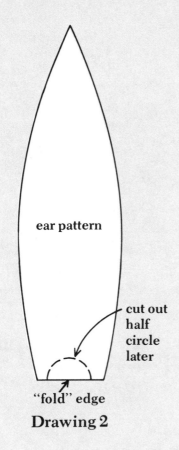

ear pattern

cut out
half
circle
later

"fold" edge

Drawing 2

Trace the ear pattern, Drawing 2. Fold a sheet of black paper in half. Tape the tracing to the paper with the edge marked "fold" touching the fold in the paper. Now fold a sheet of pink paper in half and put it inside the black paper. Drawing 3.

With the paper folded closed, cut out all three sheets—tracing paper, black paper, and pink paper—at the same time. Drawing 4. Cut about ¼ inch off the black ears, all around, to make them a little smaller than the pink ears. Open up both sets of ears. Glue the black ears on the pink ears, and refold in the middle. With the ears folded, cut out the half circle shown in Drawing 2. Unfold again and place the ears on the top of the cone as shown in the photograph.

With a pencil, punch three holes on each side of the nose. Put broom straws through these holes—in one side and out the other—for whiskers. Now glue a cotton ball on the back for a tail.

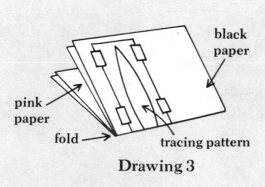

pink
paper

black
paper

fold →

tracing pattern

Drawing 3

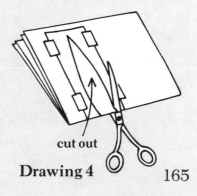

cut out

Drawing 4

Easter Egg Doll

Materials: large egg; newspapers; egg carton; yellow yarn; poster paint; masking tape; white glue. Tools: cooking pan and stove to boil egg; felt-tip markers; scissors; paintbrush; small board. Optional: brad (nail with a small head) and hammer.

CAN YOU COOK an egg and braid hair? As you make this little Dutch girl for your table, let her teach you how.

The egg should be hard-boiled. If you don't already have a hard-boiled egg, here's how to make one:

Put the egg in a cooking pan and add enough cold water to cover the egg. Put the pan on a stove burner turned to medium heat. Let the water come to a boil, then lower the heat until the water is just barely boiling. Keep the egg in the simmering water for 15 minutes. Then fill the pan with cold water. Take the egg out and let it cool.

Cover your work space with newspapers.

Hold the egg with the pointed end down. Draw a face on it with felt-tip markers. Drawing 1.

Cut out two of the cups of an egg carton, leaving the edges of the cups on. Drawing 2.

Cut one cup's edges off evenly so that it will stand upside down. Cut a hole in the top of the cup big enough to hold the egg firmly. Drawing 3.

To make a cap, cut away some of the side of the second cup and trim the edges so they are neat. Drawing 4.

Paint the cap and stand with poster paint.

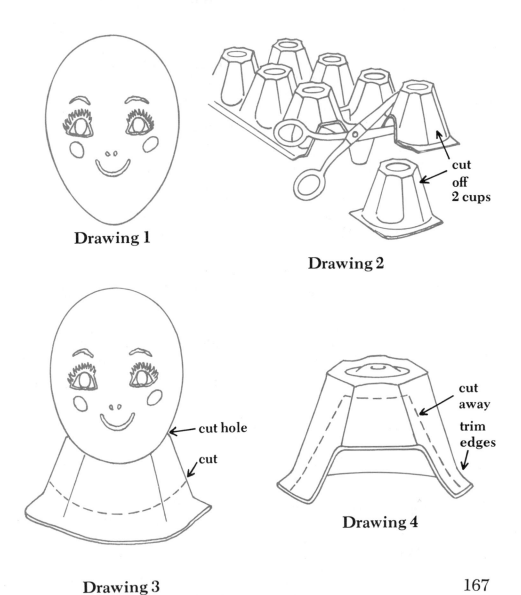

Drawing 1

cut
off
2 cups

Drawing 2

cut hole

cut

cut
away

trim
edges

Drawing 4

Drawing 3

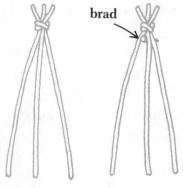

brad

Drawing 5   **Drawing 6**

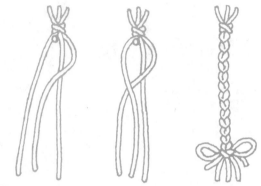

Drawing 7   **Drawing 8**   **Drawing 9**

To make braids, cut three strands of yarn, each 6 inches long. Knot the three together at one end. Drawing 5.

Tape the knotted end very firmly to a board. Or hammer a brad into a board, and put the knot over the brad. Drawing 6.

Begin braiding by bringing the right-hand strand of yarn over the middle strand. Drawing 7.

Then bring the left-hand strand over the *new* middle strand. Drawing 8.

Continue braiding, bringing the right-hand and then the left-hand strand over the middle strand. To hold the braid, knot a piece of yarn around it near the end. Tie a bow over the knot. Drawing 9. Then take the braid off the brad.

Make a second braid the same way.

Tape the braids to the top of the head. Drawing 10.

Glue the Dutch cap over the braids.

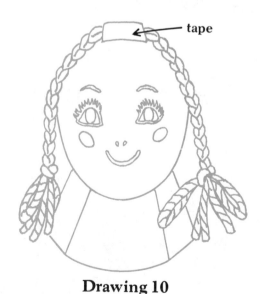

tape

Drawing 10

Halloween Patterns

Pages 184 and 185 show how to trace and transfer patterns.

169

Sad-Glad Pumpkin

Materials: newspapers to cover work space; medium-weight cardboard; white glue; orange yarn; black construction paper. Tools: pencil; scissors; brown crayon; thumbtack.

WHEN YOU'RE NOT WITH HIM, this pumpkin turns sad-side-out. To make him glad this Halloween:

Draw the outline of a pumpkin on cardboard and cut it out. The pumpkin should be about 7 inches wide and 6 inches high.

Squeeze out a strip of glue about ½ inch wide along one side of the pumpkin, on both back and front. See Drawing 1. Wind orange yarn around and around the glued area to cover it completely. Drawing 2.

Continue gluing and winding in half-inch strips until the whole pumpkin is covered with yarn—except for the stem.

With a brown crayon, color both sides of the stem.

Using black construction paper, cut six triangles and two half-moons. Glue three triangles on each side of the pumpkin for eyes and a nose. Then glue the half-moons on as shown in the two photographs.

With a thumbtack, punch a hole in the stem near the top. Enlarge the hole with a pencil. Thread a piece of orange yarn through for a hanger.

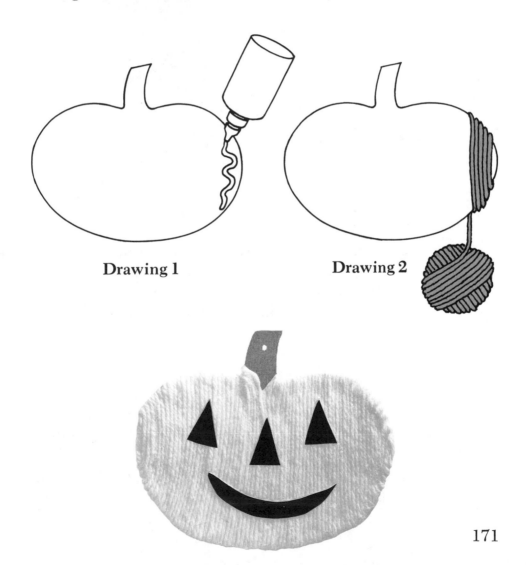

Drawing 1   Drawing 2

Cork
Halloween Favors

Materials: newspapers to cover work space; two corks, each about 2 inches high and ¾ inch across; black construction paper; white glue; toothpicks; black poster paint. **Tools:** black felt-tip marker; scissors; paintbrush; ruler; pencil; spool; food can.

WHAT'S HALLOWEEN WITHOUT BLACK CATS and witches on broomsticks? To make them appear on your Halloween table, do this magic act with corks:

With a black felt-tip marker, draw a cat face on the small end of a cork. See Drawing 1.

Cut two black ears from construction paper and glue them on. Drawing 2.

Stick in toothpicks for the legs and tail as shown in the photograph.

Paint the body, legs, and tail black.

To make the witch's cloak, cut out a piece of black construction paper measuring 3 inches by 3 inches. (Page 180 shows how.) Fold it in half, and cut as shown in Drawing 3. Unfold and then fold over the tab. Glue the tab to the top of a cork. Drawing 4.

On black construction paper draw a circle about twice as wide as the top of the cork. You can use a spool of thread as a guide. Cut out the circle and glue onto the cork over the cloak tab. Drawing 5.

Drawing 1

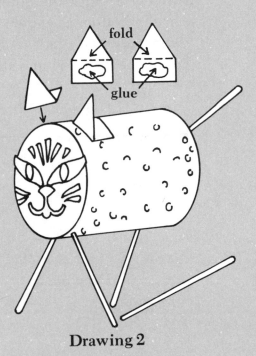

Drawing 2

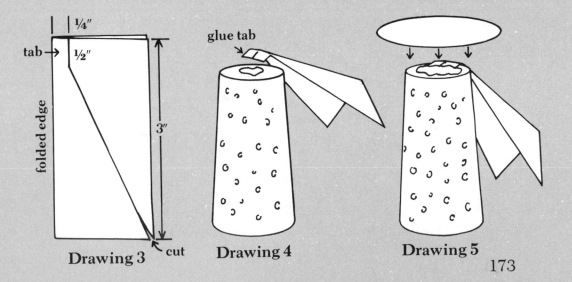

Drawing 3   **Drawing 4**   **Drawing 5**

Draw a half circle about 3 inches across. Drawing 6. You can use a can as a guide. Cut the circle out and make it into a cone. (Page 183 shows how.) Glue the cone on top of the circle to make the witch's hat.

Cut out a square measuring 1 inch by 1 inch. Fold it in half and cut diagonally from corner to corner, as shown in Drawing 7. Unfold and glue it to the end of a toothpick for a broom. Drawing 8. Stick the other end of the toothpick into the cork near the bottom as shown in Drawing 9.

Draw a witch's face on the cork with a felt-tip marker. Paint the rest of the body and the broomstick handle black.

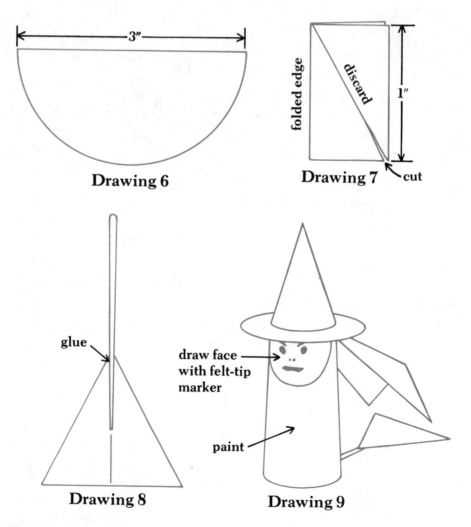

Drawing 6

Drawing 7

Drawing 8

Drawing 9

Valentine Patterns

Pages 184 and 185 show how to trace and transfer patterns.

Heart Mobile

Materials: newspapers to cover work space; white paper; lightweight cardboard; tape; red tissue paper; white glue; twine; wire coat hanger with cardboard tube crossbar; moderately heavy wire about 12 inches long. Tools: pencil; scissors; foil pan; plastic straw or stick for stirring.

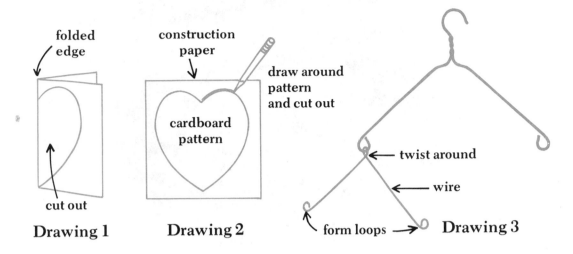

folded edge

cut out

Drawing 1

construction paper

cardboard pattern

draw around pattern and cut out

Drawing 2

twist around

wire

form loops

Drawing 3

A MOBILE is a moving sculpture. A puff of air or a gentle touch will make it dance. Here is how to make a heart mobile for Valentine's Day—or for any other day:

Fold a sheet of white paper in half. Draw half a heart at the fold, making the pattern 6 inches high. Cut it out and unfold the paper. See Drawing 1. Tape the heart to a piece of lightweight cardboard and cut out the cardboard around the heart. Drawing 2.

Using the cardboard heart as a pattern, make four tissue hearts following the same directions given for the stained-glass window ornament on pages 81–83.

Print the letters L O V E about 3 inches tall, on white paper. Cut them out and glue one letter in the center of each heart. With a pencil, punch a small hole in the top of each heart.

Remove the cardboard tube from a wire coat hanger and discard. Push down the sides of the hanger slightly to bring the hooked ends closer together. Twist a piece of 12-inch wire around one end of the hanger and form loops at each end of this wire. Drawing 3. Thread strings of different lengths through the hearts and tie the strings to the wires as shown in the photograph.

Tie a piece of string to the hook of the coat hanger. Tie a loop at the other end of this string. Use the loop to hang your mobile.

Tissue
Ornaments

Materials: construction paper; tracing paper; masking tape; colored tissue paper; yarn. Tools: pencil; scissors; stapler. Optional: carbon paper; paper punch.

STRING UP SOME TISSUE ORNAMENTS for Valentine's Day or Christmas or birthdays. To put them together:

Fold a piece of construction paper in half.

Trace one of the designs shown in Drawing 1 and transfer it to the construction paper. (Pages 184 and 185 show how.) Be sure the straight edge of the design is exactly on the fold. Drawing 2.

Cut out and unfold. Place 14 pieces of tissue paper under the

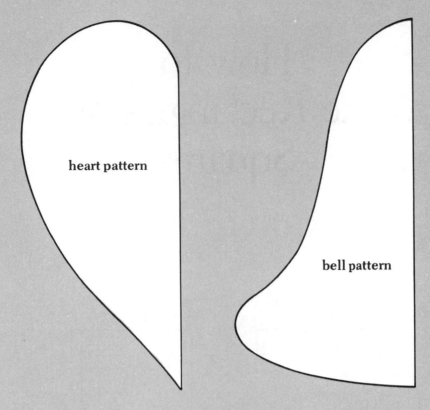

heart pattern

bell pattern

Drawing 1

construction paper and staple along the fold. Don't staple at the very top; later, you will punch a hole here. Cut the tissue out so that it is the same shape as the construction paper. Drawing 3.

Punch a hole in the top, thread yarn through, and make a loop for hanging. If you don't have a paper punch, ask an older person to make the hole with a pencil.

Separate each tissue leaf from the next to fluff out the ornament. Crease each leaf along the staples so that it will stay separate.

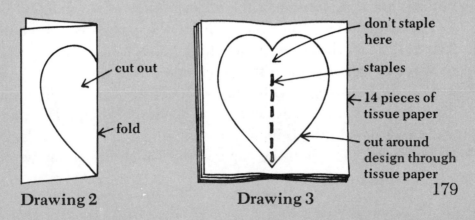

cut out

fold

don't staple here

staples

14 pieces of tissue paper

cut around design through tissue paper

Drawing 2

Drawing 3

179

How to
Make Rectangles and
Squares

Materials: paper. Tools: pencil; ruler; scissors.

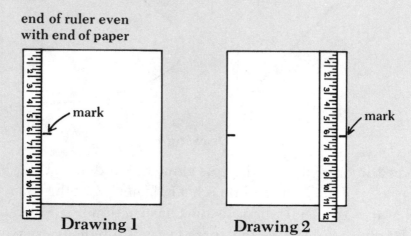

end of ruler even
with end of paper

mark

mark

Drawing 1   **Drawing 2**

Rectangles

A rectangle is a shape with four straight sides. To make one, first decide how big you want it to be. In the example here, the size is 3 inches by 6 inches. If you want your rectangle to be some other size, substitute the other numbers for the 3 and 6.

Place the ruler along one side of the paper as shown in Drawing 1. Mark the paper next to the 6-inch line on the ruler.

Move the ruler over to the other side of the paper until it is very near the edge, leaving only a thin strip of paper showing. Keep the end of the ruler even with the top of the paper. Mark the paper next to the 6-inch line. Drawing 2.

Now mark the top of the paper at the 3-inch line as shown in

180

Drawing 3. Then move the ruler down so that its top edge rests on the two 6-inch marks you made earlier. With the end of the ruler even with the left-hand edge of the paper, mark the paper at the 3-inch line. Drawing 4.

Draw a line from the left-hand edge to the mark you have just made, using the ruler as a guide. Drawing 5. Now draw a line joining the two 3-inch marks. Drawing 6.

Cut out the rectangle along the two lines. Drawing 7.

Squares

A square is a special kind of rectangle—all four of its sides are the same length. You make squares in the same way as other rectangles.

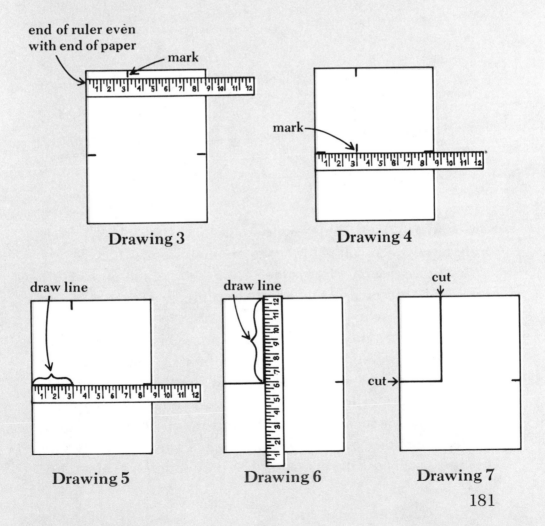

Drawing 3

Drawing 4

Drawing 5

Drawing 6

Drawing 7

How to Make Circles and Cones

Materials for circles: paper. Tools: pencil; ruler; compass, or round objects, or thumbtack and string; medium-weight cardboard. To make cones you will also need tape.

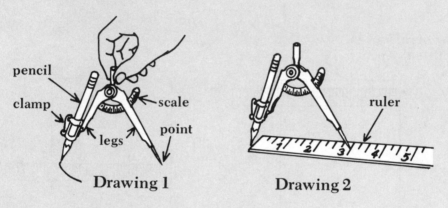

Drawing 1　　　　　**Drawing 2**

Circles

A compass is a drawing instrument that will make a perfect circle of any size you want, up to about 10 inches across.

A compass has two legs. One is pointed and the other has a clamp to hold a pencil. You hold the pointed leg at the center of the circle and swing the pencil leg around to draw the circle. Drawing 1. Put a piece of cardboard under your drawing paper first, so that the pointed end doesn't scratch your table. The scale on the compass shows about how big the circle will be.

The best way to make a circle the size you want is to use a ruler, as shown in Drawing 2. Spread the pencil leg and the pointed leg of the compass apart on the ruler until they mark off *half* the size (*half* the diameter) of the circle you want. For instance, to make a circle 6 inches across, spread the compass legs 3 inches apart.

If you don't have a compass, you can use a round object as a pattern for your circle. For instance, you can use a coin, a drinking glass, a plate, a jar top, or a can. Drawing 3.

To make very large circles, you can use a thumbtack and a piece of string, as shown in Drawing 4.

Cones

Decide how big you want your cone to be. Let's say you want the bottom, or base, of your cone to be 3 inches across—to have a 3-inch diameter. You will need a sheet of paper at least twice that wide and four times that long. The paper will have to be at least 6 inches wide and 12 inches long.

Draw a half circle with a diameter of 12 inches. Drawing 5. Cut out the half circle. Bring the two corners together, slipping one under the other. Drawing 6. Now roll the cone tighter, keeping the corners at the top rim, until the corners meet again. Tape the seam. Drawing 7.

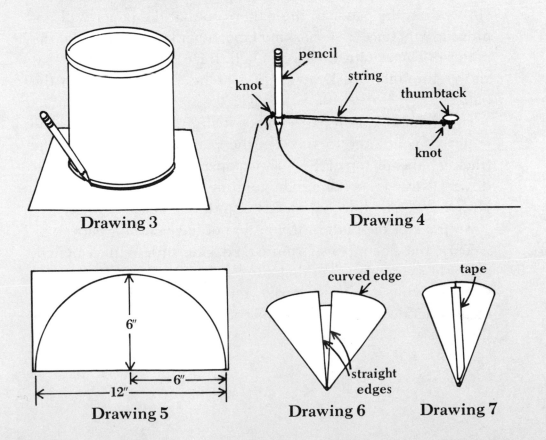

Drawing 3

pencil

knot   string

thumbtack

knot

Drawing 4

6″

6″

12″

Drawing 5

curved edge

straight edges

Drawing 6

tape

Drawing 7

How to
Trace and Transfer
a Pattern

Materials: tracing paper; working material—paper, cardboard, or cloth; masking tape. Tools: pencil. Optional: carbon paper.

You can transfer a pattern or picture from any book or magazine to your own material. You can transfer it to paper, cardboard, or cloth.

Lay the tracing paper over the pattern (or picture) you want to copy. Tape the paper to the pattern so that the paper will not move as you trace. Use masking tape; other kinds might tear the pattern. Then, with a sharp pencil, trace over every line that shows through. See Drawing 1. Untape the tracing from the pattern.

If you have carbon paper, place it shiny side down over the material you want to transfer the pattern to. Then lay the tracing paper on top of the carbon paper. Tape the tracing paper down. Now trace along the outline on the tracing paper. Drawing 2. The lines will transfer to the material. Untape.

To transfer the pattern if you do not have carbon paper:

Turn the tracing over (unmarked side up). With a pencil, scribble over every line that shows through from the marked side. Drawing 3. (If the material you are going to put the pattern on is a dark color, use chalk instead of pencil to scribble over the lines.)

184

Then turn the tracing paper marked-side-up again. Lay it on the material you want to put the pattern on. Tape the tracing and material together. With a sharp pencil, go over the lines of the pattern again. The lines will transfer to the material. Drawing 4.

Untape the tracing. If the lines on the material are very faint, draw along them to darken them. Drawing 5.

pattern showing through paper

tracing paper   tape

Drawing 1

carbon paper, shiny side down   tape

tracing paper

material receiving pattern

Drawing 2

Drawing 3

tracing paper

material receiving pattern

Drawing 4

Drawing 5

Hints on Tools, Materials, and Supplies

Tools

The essentials are pencils, a ruler, scissors (the blunt type for younger children), and paintbrushes of various sizes. Also useful are the following:

Compass. An inexpensive compass holding a short wooden pencil will do. But use with caution—the sharp metal point can be dangerous for younger children and, even when used by older children, can punch holes in your table tops.

Paper Punch. This item is not essential, but it will make some projects easier and neater. It will also produce small circles of paper to be used as decorations—but be prepared to find these small circles all over the house.

Stapler. Few projects in this book call for a stapler, but in other projects it can often become an easier substitute for tape or glue. Not for younger children unless they are supervised.

Adhesives and Tapes

White Glue (such as "Elmer's" brand) is a must. It will stick to most surfaces, is easy to apply, and—if caught before it dries—can be washed off surfaces and out of clothing. It comes out of the container in a string (much like toothpaste) and requires a small piece of cardboard (such as a matchbook cover or file card) to spread evenly. Mixed with an equal amount of water (in an aluminum foil pan) it forms a base for making papier-mâché.

186

Paste has fewer uses than white glue and can form lumps. Younger children, however, generally find it easier to use.

Plastic Cement, obtainable from hobby shops, is the only kind of glue that will adhere to certain plastics. It should be used only under adult supervision.

Transparent Tape (such as "Scotch" brand) is, like white glue, a must. There are two kinds—glossy and matte. Pencil and crayon will not adhere to the glossy type. Matte tape is more expensive, but crayon and pencil will adhere.

Masking Tape is a brown, self-adhesive paper tape. It is usually wider than transparent tape and holds better when there are stresses. It can be removed without tearing away part of the surface to which it was stuck—thus making it useful for taping down tracing paper or taping objects to a wall. It is the least expensive of all self-adhesive tapes. All kinds of paints and colors will adhere.

Colors

Crayons and Felt-tip Markers. Felt-tip markers come in a variety of vivid colors, adhere to most surfaces, and have many general household uses as well as craft uses. There are two types—indelible and water-soluble. Be sure to get the latter. Crayons are less versatile than felt-tip markers, but much less expensive and are more suitable for younger children.

Watercolors come in metal containers, each holding a number of colors in compartments. Their use requires frequent dabs of the brush into water and they are unsuitable for painting large areas. Poster paints are more satisfactory for most uses.

Poster Paints (also called tempera colors) are water-soluble and easy to clean up. Each color comes in its own small bottle, but you can buy packages of several colors (usually green, yellow, blue, red, white, and black). Poster paints will cover larger areas than watercolors, are easier to use, and provide a denser covering, but are somewhat messier. Widely used in nursery schools. Waterbase wall paints, left over from your last decorating job, can be used as a substitute.

Plastic-model Paints (such as "Testor's" brand), obtainable from hobby stores, come in tiny jars and are relatively expensive. They are needed for painting plastics and will stick to most other surfaces as well. They provide a glossy finish. A bottle of thinner is required to clean the brush.

Enamel Paint. A few of the projects in this book require enamel paint to adhere to the surfaces used. This paint should be used under adult supervision because spillage can be a disaster and stains in clothing are permanent. Turpentine or thinner is needed to clean the brushes and hands. The price of this paint is relatively high, so it is best to use leftovers from household paint jobs. Spray paint, which comes in small cans, is not recommended for children.

Shellac. The applying of shellac is an optional finishing touch that should be done only under adult supervision. Thinner is needed to clean the brushes.

Paper

Construction Paper is useful for many projects. It comes in three basic sizes—9 by 12 inches, 12 by 18 inches, and 18 by 24 inches. You can buy a package of mixed colors (usually black, white, orange, red, yellow, green, blue, and pink) or of a single color. It can easily be cut with blunt scissors.

Typing or Notebook Paper is useful for patterns and for the finished product of certain projects. For these purposes, use a heavyweight typing paper, not tissue. Lined notebook paper is readily available if you have school-age children and, because of the lines, is easier to use when drawing or cutting geometric shapes.

Tracing Paper can be bought in rolls, sheets, or pads; pads are recommended. You can also use lightweight (tissue) typing paper. Used with carbon paper, tracing paper will have many uses beyond those mentioned in this book.

Carbon Paper, although not essential for transferring patterns (see page 184 for an alternate method), is a great convenience. (But it does smear fingers.) Stationery stores generally stock a special carbon paper for pencils, but regular typewriter carbon will also work.

Crepe Paper and Tissue Paper. These two papers can often serve the same purposes. Crepe paper, however, is easier to cut and apply; also, crepe paper stretches, while tissue paper tears easily. Both papers come in a wide variety of colors. Crepe paper comes in long, folded sheets, usually 20 inches wide. The size of tissue paper varies greatly.

Gift-wrapping Paper is useful for outside coverings and decorations. Save partial rolls and scraps.

Brown Paper can be bought in rolls (generally about 3 feet wide) or you can make your own by cutting apart grocery bags. Useful for projects where oversize sheets are needed.

Cardboard

Lightweight. Use file cards, file folders, tag board, bristol board, or lightweight poster board. Tag board, bristol board, and poster board can be purchased at stationery or art-supply stores. Lightweight poster board is also available at many variety stores. Tag board (also called oak tag board) is creamy-yellow and generally comes in sheets measuring 24 by 36 inches. Bristol board is white and comes in somewhat smaller sheets. Lightweight poster board comes in white and various colors, usually in 22 by 28 inch sheets. Specify lightweight (about $1/32$ inch thick) because there are heavier grades.

Medium-weight. Use shirt cardboard, gift boxes, or 14-ply poster board. You can buy 14-ply poster board at stationery or art-supply stores. White sheets generally measure 40 by 60 inches. Smaller sheets in vivid colors are also available.

Yarn

Four-ply Yarn—the kind used in ordinary knitting—is meant whenever this material is specified.

Index

This index lists the kinds of things to make and the kinds of activities described. Basic materials are also included, in bold type, so that you can find uses for household objects and for leftovers from previous projects. (Such items as fasteners, adhesives, and paints are omitted)